*Also by Peter O'Leary*

POETRY

*Earth Is Best*

*The Sampo*

*Phosphorescence of Thought*

*Luminous Epinoia*

*Depth Theology*

*Watchfulness*

PROSE

*The Four Horsemen: Poetry and Apocalypse*

*Thick and Dazzling Darkness: Religious Poetry in a Secular Age*

*Gnostic Contagion: Robert Duncan & the Poetry of Illness*

AS EDITOR

Ronald Johnson

*Collected Later Poems*

*The Book of the Green Man*

*ARK*

*Radi os*

*The Shrubberies*

*To Do as Adam Did: Selected Poems*

John Taggart

*Is Music: Selected Poems*

# THE
# HIDDEN
# EYES
## OF
# THINGS

STUDIES FOR THE
ADVANCEMENT OF
THE SACRO-MAGICAL
SCIENCES NO. 2

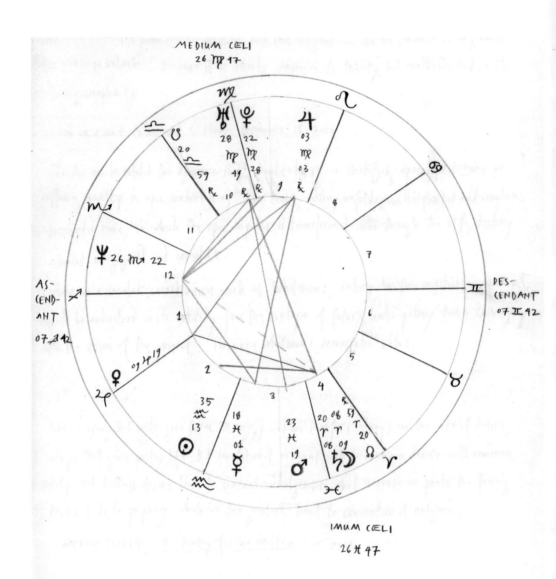

MEDIUM CŒLI
26 ♍ 17

AS-
CEND-
ANT

07 ♐ 42

DES-
CENDANT
07 ♊ 42

IMUM CŒLI
26 ♓ 47

SATURDAY, FEBRUARY 3, 1968

3:30 AM, EASTERN STANDARD TIME / 8:30 UNIVERSAL TIME

PETROIT, MICHIGAN 42N20 / 83W03

SUN SIGN, AQUARIUS      ASCENDANT, SAGITTARIUS

# THE HIDDEN EYES OF THINGS

PETER O'LEARY

THE CULTURAL SOCIETY

BROOKLYN

MMXXII

FOR GABBY (FIRE)
AND LUCIAN (AIR)

*Astrological superstition is based upon the obscure feeling of an immense universe.*

—Goethe to Schiller, December 8, 1798

*And sawst the secrets of the world vnmade.*

—*Faerie Queene* I.v.22.6

THE

# HIDDEN

# EYES

OF

# THINGS

# AN ARGUMENT

## (MILTON 2016)

The Arch-chimic Sun. Its vectorial fires
a serpent thickens in whose
salamandrine choir hisses like fat.

We believed resentment a form of prophecy.
We railed against the tyranny of Heaven.
We formed a great republic.

Now fools turn lies to gold and transformation
is a law in politics only. Satan
sheds his rind of scales, his new skin

aglister like oiled seeds. They should
destroy us now. With daggers hacked
from the broken limbs of the Tree of Life,

the ones we burn for fuel. Or better yet,
its unsung fruit whose bitter pit
we'd choke on like a philosopher's stone.

# MASTERS OF TIME

In the ninth, a lulling angelic lunacy.
In the eighth, thaumaturgy's archangelic quicksilver.
In the seventh, passion's volcanic principality.
In the sixth, the Sun's stunning magicum.
In the fifth, a dynamo's martial quintessence.
In the fourth, dominion's lordly fortunes.
In the third, a throne of woe.
In the second, a fire-formed Promethean cosmism.
In the first, the mover's Seraphic origin.
And the last, imagination's empyreal zero.

○

# OMEN

Look.
The Sun is total gold.
Mercury is liquid thought in blinks of lightning.
Venus in copper shows her radiant face early and late.

The Moon is chaste silver.

Mars is an iron bane, always looming never coinciding.

Jupiter shines brightest of all against a ceiling of hammered tin.

Saturn of the antique law is distant to the eyes drawing

a heavy thumb of gloom

across the lead of the sky he has shaded with a black

bile of space, atoms

in embryo.


Rebellion scorches through the fixed stars.

The First Mover's feeling is oceanic.

A cool plutonic gaze overlooks an empire of frozen fire.


*God wants to be born in the flame of consciousness*, torching

all the wretched straw on the floor of the manger.

Will you be an advocate of the Earth?


In a gulf of sleep a torque of gold

sits atop a wandering fire

consuming you from head to foot,

an oracle no burning cleans.


Great watery influx.

The sea bursting through the narrow gates of the stars.

Rowdy swells of the mother-sea.

Wounded arm of the mother-sea.

Turbid surging mirror of the mother-sea.

Struck aqueous crystal of the primum mobile.
Dodecatropaic gash of the stars.
Detonating nuclear serpent power writhing through matter awakened
in the sexual gasp of an insight.

The universe is not a vast machine.
It's an astro-neurology.
A science of feeling and stars.
Transmitting messages from fringe to center and back again.
Catapulted. Gushed. Ended. Rebegun.

>   *The waters of earth*
>   *a broth of ghosts—*
>
>   *the stars an antique*
>   *robe of earth.*

Look.
The towering thistle has
stinging thatches
that show you in growth
those stellar networks hatching galaxies
like the abundant spiky lobes
of the thistle's pale purple blooms, an epic
fizz of noise bees
cling to while finches
thrash the pillowy puffs of the seeds to tatters.

Look, then.
On the shining glory forming from
tonned atom to Sun showering outward
its hell of light a cream of night
cools into a radiant circuit of living forms
from the visible relics
of the sky's dark laws.

*O zodion kyklos*
*a mercy fastness.*

Look.
The zodiac's encincturing band dials heaven,
measuring time.
Or seems to.
Whose vistas draw limits to a converging movement
streams of concentration whirl down into.
What if the zodiac represents not an outer limit, a band
beyond which the Empyrean blazes in all its glory,
but a reflective limit,
the ecliptical mirror
redirecting the spiritual gaze
inward
to its volatile core
of potable gold?

Look.
A more precise knowledge of the motions of all the stars

and the Sun and the Moon—
the state of the appearances of things—
there is nothing small or accidental about causes.

The universe is an intelligent environment—

the genius Sun
the roaring Earth
beneath your feet
moist honey
on your tongue.

Ptolemy's aeonic rotations
the stars in daemonic torment forecast

unmirror the Nemesis slipping its orbit
who moves in menace unspinning

to blot
all fate.

Say:
*Lords*—
*you ruling the disturbingly animated depths*
*and you shades in the zero's oracle;*
*you Chaos and you Phlegethon ruling night's unechoing hollows*
*and you spirit forces in the void cone of sleep:*
*Let me say what I've heard,*

*what the massive sulking earth makes darkness from,*
*what numinous abyss it hides, what*
*secrets buried unfold there.*
*What's worth telling.*

You are the disciple of your discipline, contouring
its precessive, morphomatic drag
into a radiating, twelve-formed circlet
pulled
in both aura
and core
at once,

a universe,
*a triple abyss of stars and atoms and generation,*
its immensity intuited.

FROM THE SPECTACLE

OF YOUR IMAGINATION,

ITS BIRTH

A young ram with its horns locked in the thorns of the Burning Bush
straining in the Moon's cooling light that midnight stains blue.

# THE STROKES OF THE MOON

Shining fog. Loose and purling. Can you feel the scene?
It's your soul, total, growing
strange tusks.

The sulfureous Sun is underneath the Earth.
The opaque globe of the Moon, the curving shoulders of the virgin,
clouded with storms.
Where is your
daemonic core? Nature's
cryptic physics psychic depths unbind: You
are not intelligent but divinity
in you
is.

An unthundering smoke
fills into itself
drawn across your field of vision—eerie
with silver moonlight. Beyond
you know how stars are born and how they die. Beyond
the stars obey the dark law
the Moon outshines that your heart

picks up every ricocheting echo of, light
tapping out every pulse of moonlit
time.

River of silver, flow!
River of argenteous electricity, rush and flow!
Restless, peaceless influx, flow!
River of soul that pours into the reservoir of your depths, paroxysmal and
    mesmeric, push on!
River of shining life.
River of dark fate.
Daemonic, dynamic river of moonlight
sound to the soul the powers of life,
the unsettled anguishes of life.

The Moon is not dead but only sleeps.
*Of all causes, the remotest are the stars*; the nearest
the insane
maternal Moon.

Bright Moon, white Moon
radiant as an elf and as strange.
Shining Moon garmented in feathers, silver aura of wings—
Lore's daughters and Time's wards sing her song.
Upheaven's encircling sheen of silk elven bale outfires
as Earth's umbering temperatures smolder.
*Who says the Absence of a Witch invalidates his spell?*

Air's blazeless lift beams coronal gold elf-shine pearls

whose sparks light her shape when she rises from the brim of the stream,

her bathstead in a broth of dusk where she tenses the reins of the horses of
   night.

Deep-maned horses speeding forward, twilight's shadow set on fire,

smoke of silver coloring another world.

Bright Moon, silver Moon,

radiant as an elf and as strange.


Do you hear me calling in the night, Moon in the sky with unusual wings?

Wilderness silver and underworld smoke

flash through the twilight in tattered enamel—

elf-shine and menace, Moon fruit and spectacle.

You sense order in things in all sorts of places—is this

the form that makes the universe like God?

Arcing stars. Liquid night.

Geysering Moon, its aura of horror.

Geysering Moon, its sterling jets.

Geysering Moon, its frost of chrome

burning midheaven's ensuing night

the saturnine chronocrator suffuses with woe.

World historical, judgmental woe.


The Moon's initial condition of moisture.

The Moon's eventual densifying plasmas.

The Moon's atmospheric fire fog.

The cadre of angels overseeing the Old Moon's phase of life.

Can spells pull down the Moon from the heavens?

Stellatus in the Moon's diadem.

The Moon's daemonic lymph.

What is the hue of the Moon in the elements?

The feline Sun must be purring as it combusts.


The Moon's silver lunation slips like a sylph through the night.

The Moon's silver frost.

The baleful moondew used by the witches of Thessaly.

The Moon's blue shining of the sky's starry gates.

Great, frightening, nocturnal columns of the Moon's illumination.

A newborn ruminant's life of the Moon capering on the feeling of a rocky
   upslope.

The Sun created in a single blessedness; the Moon in the cohering onslaught
   of an afterthought.

The Moon's calligraphy of revelation.

The Moon's Mare Imbrium, vast and smooth and flooded with antique lava.

The Moon's unusual historical residues.

Artemis enclouded by lascivious quails.

The Moon's diffusion of the visible and invisible.

The Moon's centripetal immanence.

The Moon's syringing tidal resonance.

The Moon's annual tidal bore.

The Moon's riverine wall of water.

The Moon's gestating spring tides, its unconscious neap tides.

The Moon's phlegmatic selenoscope.

The Moon *cluttered with filth and wild beasts*.

Rising in front of you, a great circle
but entirely black, as it were a tar compounded with silver.
Revealed in agony. Declarer of magic. Who
is the magus of the Moon? Someone
who is writing the trilogies, surely.


Colored photisms of the visionary ascent. Will you
climb the ladder into the middle realm of silvers?
Light of speech
light of hearing
supersensory light of the selenodonts feeling the darkness
with the ridges of their molars. What
are the lunatic species they prey on?


Circle of the tarry darkness.
Circle of the vital *pneuma*.
Alphabet engendered by the heaven of the Moon—
alphabetic lunar phases, including two pauses, two silences—
The Hour
is upon you. The Moon
has been cloven.


The Moon's daring crescent caught in the horns of the midwinter ram
the night's deepest portion strains the moods of
above the labyrinthine
House of the Mother
in which

your life
is wound.


Brother, you've seen some monstrous things
in the silvery Moon's quintessential light
reknown there in your feelings like
ribs in a cage, engraved
by the maternal hand a generational disappointment
endures in, stroke by judgmental
stroke.


*Do you hear me calling in the night, Moon in the sky with unusual wings?*
Moon in the sky, you wilderness of silver.
Moon in the sky censing the underworld with your alluring and myrrhy
	smoke of blue.


The Moon's predictive moistures.
The Moon's visionary rumor, floating above the abdomen of a medium.
The moon's nighttime pneumatism.


A torpid lunar drowse comes over you, moist as moonlight, mild
and reminiscent of your mother, the mansion
in whose Fourth House your incarnating soul
entered the physical realm,
the whole experience preceding birth a torrent
of hidden things the hearth of life
enearths in kith
and ancient kin

in a dream Ptolemy
smoothed into radiant spheres.

*Of all causes, the remotest are the stars.*

You wander alone in the magnificent emptiness
of the silver lunar mansion the daughters of night
sprinkle with white sulfur, arcanest
substance.

Bountiful nurse of the dew.
Sap of the water of life.
Philosophical ichor.

What are your memories of sickness and health?
A morphine of sleep interrupts them.
Have you ever dreamt of a moon-plant, a mandrake
or fungus of lethal design?
A feminine conjunction would show forth the Dipper—
its seven stars like Ptolemy's dream.

Your dream of the moon is a dream of your mother
and you are a wind she carried in her belly,
a silver she warmed into sulfuric cream.

*If you do me no hurt, oh Moon.*
Clothed with your blackness, the matrimonial wrangle.
The eclipse of the Sun-fed lion.

Eternal.

Ethereal.

Ephemeral.

Sublunar world we drowse in—a lower world.

Perishable realm.

Loveliness of the new Moon enveiling her dark side, far-

finding eye of the mediatrix, partaker

of Earth's sufferings and its daemonic

darkness as well.


From a distance,

you are entrusted with building a summertime

temple for your mother.


She is lying there,

you can see her, absorbing the northern sunlight, slowly

in the languorous daylight of the lengthening hours curing her skin

to a nut-brown color, lying there

in the park on a lawn chair on the grass

next to a picnic table, the lake

puddling out from behind her


while you and your brothers

and your cousin and all of your friends

stream through the park to the pool—what else

is there to do in July? There she remains through the day in the Sun,

reading and chatting, the Sun's hierogamous suppliant.

But it's the hollowness, the absorptive
passive principle of the moonlight
that nourishes you. Not the Sun's
life-giving radiance but the Moon's
transient reflectiveness.
You're aware
even then
of her sorrow,
the simplex
of never having been sufficiently loved
by her own mother, a matter
she will always overcompensate for by loving you
into these complex entanglements, the very
mesh from which
you will build this illustrious temple
and whose design
you can never entirely contemplate
not even now, after all these years

like the Moon's own *magnificent desolation*
or Titan's encompassing atmosphere dense
with blue methane. Mortification

and understanding—these
twist in your imagination like
great
tethering
braids.

But she's a survivor after all, despite
the weak valence
of the love she received, pulling
whatever force she owns into the colossal tides of her mothering, exopathic
and weather-like. Deep source
of all your dreams. You are aware
at last of all the energy your father
absorbed from her, how
demanding his needs, how evaporative
his actions. A man for whom joy
has been a hardship despite his worldly successes, despite
his fortune in having her there.

So where does it come from? All the goodness you feel?
From the Moon. Funneling into you
its extraordinary zodiacal light
of silver and ire.

CODA

The dragon.
The serpent.
The scorpion.
The toad.
The basilisk.
The lion.
The bear.

The wolf.
The dog.
The eagle.
The raven.

The fox
and the junco.
The alchemical novilunium
and the souls
streaming
from on high
down into the lower realms.

The stone
flattened by time's watery action.
The stone in your hand
and the stone on the book.
The stone on your tongue
and the stone in your throat
the folds of your tonsils
shape from sulfureous ash
into
the horns
of the Moon.

FROM THE SPECTACLE
OF YOUR IMAGINATION,
ITS NERVOUS SYSTEM

Mercury's hypochondriacal fickleness unspooling the silver cord
joining the fish aswim in the night's third hour.

# YOUR LEFT HAND
# SHEATHED IN
# QUICKSILVER

*et clamavit voce magna*


### LITURGY OF CRYSTAL

Chrome in mercury the archangelic sigh.
Animate the body in quicksilver's
wink.

You sense it.
Falling apart. The convolutions.
You've become aware of a shape in occultation—
an orbital resonance,
a nemesis
held in abeyance, a menace.
Telling you that things are falling apart.
Foreknown, manifested. *Ego sum alpha et omega, principium et finis*—
for revelation is an alphabetic, an
exegetical totality, tasting of alchemical starch and eschatological nickel.

Deeper knowledge, its inner earth, licit prime—
these heaven handed over. Colossal shaping of the stars. Secret of the skies.
  Great milk of space.
Nemesis tremoring to life in the surging warps.
Who is the thief of this wisdom, these knowings
by which things are ruled?
It is godlike to look into the shapes of the stars and know them.
Stars in smears spread through the void, over
and under the Earth at all hours. Awe roused not only by the species
but the power of things as well.
What have you seen in the epic drowse?
What spectacle in the crystal flickering vision?

You have looked in bewilderment at the strange new light of heaven.
You have been saddened by its cyclic loss, taking joy
at its rebirth. You have seen the streaming yellow shadows
in the Sun's glowing golden roar. You have
turned day into night and night into day.
You have tuned your ear to birdsong.
You have stared at the slickened entrails of animals, divining stellar portents.
You have summoned the dead whom you've aroused from the depths of the
  earth.


FOR THE ANGEL WHO ANNOUNCES THE END OF TIME

Coins, oil, the coil, the curl Raphael
the archangelic gerent pours transformed as
quicksilver from crystal his left hand

fixes with an unnumbing electrical surge. Heavens

upheaved. Flashed

in a day twice as long as a year. Roils

of hoary Sun blindness. Arithmetic

of daily movement, its toils in sunstroke.

What avatar of the unexpected flare arises in this relative turning

to the Sun? What supersensory personal master occulted

in the astral matter seethes there? What homologue to your perfect nature

do you sense there? The primordial secret. Its allure. What

bearer of darkness transforms it into a night of

light?


     By noon

on the day Mercury was born he left

his cradle and invented the lyre.


Amorous Jupiter with numerous nymphs.

Mercury's orgiastic cairn.

The flesh-sacrificing godling, darling

of heavenly forms and earthly worth. Dew

clinging to the grass blades in the pre-dawn. Masteries

coursing through the fantasies of the Fore-Time.

Mercury's auguring curiosities.

Deftly stepping god of the ways, inventor of

the game of knucklebones and the art of divining with them.

Alphabet, astronomy, musical scales, boxing and gymnastics, weights and

    measures.

Underworld conductor,

bemused manager of otherworldly things.


27

*Shepherd of thin dreams.*
*A cow-stealing, night-watching, and door-waylaying thief.*


ABYSM OF SACRIFICE


Mercury seems to be serving the Sun but
secretly serves the dark masters of knowledge in
subsystemic routines of distortion the light
floods and the mind unwrinkles.
Spring warblers' volumetric telephones of sound.
Successions of beings.
Rotations of the archangels, their
manifestations. The detriment of the retrograde.
Mercury's surge of creation as theophany.
His sophianic psalm a being of pure light.


HERMETIC LITANY


Mercury's disturbances in the harmonics of fascination.
Your mind nourished by unleavened magic.

Mercury's closeness to the massive Sun, its movement warped by undula-
    tions of relative time and space.
Mercury's intellectual lack of an atmosphere—torched by solar proximity.
Mercury's weak gravitational bombardment.

Mercury's immanent crisis slowed by atomic epoch and mass.

Mercury's engulfing in the red super giant of the Sun, the gas and dust of
the dying Sun drifting off into space forming a vast dark cloud out from
which as in a womb of black light

a new sun might take shape.


Mercury's exioherari.

Mercury the sperm of all metals.

Mercury's quicksilver fecundated by sulfur.

Mercury's detriments in the harmonics of slow time.

Mercury's ripples in the fabric of communication.

Mercury's tail in the solar stain.


Mercury lord of the birds of omen.

Mercury lord of the slit-eyed lions.

Mercury lord of all the aurochsen and bison once roaming the contours of
the good Earth.

Mercury lord who longs for the taste of flesh.


Mercury from Earth a lucid pinpoint in a penumbral pre-dawn—the hori-
zon spooked with embers from the coming Sun.

Mercury's igneous comb of craters.

Mercury whose scant atmosphere was probably captured from a solar wind,
a stream of atomic particles thrown out by the Sun.


Mercury's magnetic field of unknown origin.

Mercury's trim beard of craters.

"As seen
from some locations on the planet,
the Sun would rise, then stop, back up, and set
in the east, then rise again, move across the sky
to the west, set, rise again in the west, then
finally set."

Mercury's
disdain of moons.
Mercury's mysterious caprices of an orderliness not entirely always easily
    tracked.

Mercury's ecstasy in the archangelic sigh.
Mercury's shimmer as the mesocosm oscillates, in and out of view.
Mercury's laddered realm of all the divine names from where the Earth
    tenses in mysterious light.

Mercury's jackdaw.
Mercury's feline forepaw, broken then healed. Look! The cat's thief-like
    athletic *tigersprung*.


HYMN OF AGITATION TO THE SEVEN SPHERES

Ecstatic wounds, gash of stars,
oily sheen matter is slicked with—
who announces the end of time? The animals,
prancing through the real. You're their shepherd,

30

you lead them through the rocky passes where time
is strangely magnetized in its gravitational
onrush. Whose gravity?
The stars'? No. The Sun's above all.
Whom God summons. And who speaks,
making all things towards our end accrue.


MERCURY'S DAEMONIC MOONCLAW

Juno sends Argus with his century of eyes to watch over Io
like a Tyrolean milk cow in an alpine upland, shaggy with beatitude,
her cowbell clanking in a summer snowstorm.

Juno jealous of Jove's roving lusts tells Mercury
with his flowering virga to slay Argus—she wants
Io unguarded. Mercury
strokes a tune on his lute
lulling Argus into torpor deepening
his sleep with a wave of his
wand. One hundred eyes drawn closed for rest.

At his thick neck, where the monster's ponderous head is lolling, Mercury
flashes the falcon of his sword, a scythe-like incisor,
unburdening Argus of his head,
spraying the nearby cliffside red with gore,
great torrents of blood
mercy fitfully shuns. "Argus," says Mercury, "thou liest low;

the light which thou hadst within thy fires is all put out;
the one darkness fills thy hundred eyes."

Juno Saturn's daughter and sister to her husband Jove flames with rage
setting a terror-bearing fury in the heart of Io and then
hounding her fleeing through
all the lengths of the world.
But not before setting all of Argus's radiant eyes
in the peacock's fanning tail
so her iridescent familiar in moments of lust
might always tremor with the memory of his mistress's
betrayal.

Mercury's daemonic moonclaw, its
murderous kithness
the stars' endless acrework of dark
and light. The daystar's dawn of dread in
trouble in the rudderless age of fools
all the omens augur.

Blue crystal of daylight.
Mercurial silver of twilight, like a consonant
silent through a verb. You
are the unfashioned fashioner.
You weave the patterns of resurrection.
You enable the seasonal resurgence.
So bright in your new body.

The sky slides towards darkness the stars stipple. Who
should be wary of the fieldwork they require
to be made sense of?

Far-off throbs of thunder summer summons like rumors storms deny
before punishing the day with
damages
apocalyptic and liberating.

Through any sunstorm's upending weather
Mercury's astromantic horolation shines
like white gold burnished in the bergamot
a forewarning with feverfew's
bitter edge
fans over.


OVERWHELMING THE GAY AND LORDLY BODY

The human form became to you an index
of revelation. *Oh my brother*, you said, *truly
I have seen eleven heavens, and the Moon and the Sun.*
And you heard, from inside the chamber of your sleep an echoing voice
that said, *What you have seen
is among the bequeathings of the unbeheld that we
will show
to thee.*

In the slot of a long valley fringed
on its edges with trees leading to an outstretched
extensive upslope, the grasses cropped short as in a meadow
that has been grazed, and you are making your way up,
pulling yourself towards the top of the upslope, step by step, your brother
climbing alongside.

And the going is hard
but you're moving upwards
and gaining, feeling good despite
the great ongoing shape of cloud heaving
in an ominous uneven sheet
above. And the closer you come
the thicker
its movements, pitches but also rotations, a worrying undular
cloudhang, pendular mammary lobes in
agitated motion from gray to cream in color,
weirdstuff
in a whirling swarm.

                    Upwards
you ascend, your brother
a step or two ahead; there's a wild wind whose
coarse untipped roar reaches the end of the meadow
where the turf disappears into cloud. Roiling there
just inches above your
heads. What

secrecy yields
to the glory?


      Your brother
pierces the surging sheet of cloud
and disappears. You're alarmed. Should you follow? The thickened gauze
of cloud extends opaque in all directions. In a rush,
of a sudden, upwards you
thrust—


Gold.
A lift of light rimed with gold.
And the ringing of an all-consuming mesocosmic chord.
As if a chorus of parallel voices singing in unison at full throat.
A feeling of great kindness.
And a redolence of cedar, of juniper warmed by Ice Age light.
Everywhere that lift.
And the cloud as smooth as a sheet of gold unrolled flat
as far as you can see. Ahead,
your brother, a newly born ancient of days, wading on hands and knees.
And ahead of him, slightly upslope, others, also newly ancient, athrill in
    their
crawling higher and higher into life all
moving into the omni-radiant light
the flow of gold shakes out from
in a lavish total wave. And everywhere
an ether-clad swale of gold, its eddying sheet

swirling, its omen of light

outlandish where

foresight and

surmisal

have foreknown

this realm of wonders released,

this churning major chord,

this quicksilver wonder-clamor

hidden but for vision from view.


CODA


Ether, breath, sperm, stars.

Your pneumatic soul resembles grasses summer passes through.

Or the religious physics of the Neoplatonists.

The rotation of the universe results from consonant turning in the world-
  soul

which consists of wind and light

and magnetic echoes.

Your soul's essence is motion.

Like a flock of sparrows in erotic chase.

Or like the flash of dancing in the branches of a newly leaved honey locust.

Or like the secret of the consuming Sun, in the magnificent theopathy of its
  suicidal expansion,

that it fails entirely to reveal

even as it throbs across its white gold seals and quicksilver hinges.

FROM THE SPECTACLE

OF YOUR IMAGINATION,

ITS ENDOCRINES

Hesperian Venus vaults the horizon the Sun's beams have stained
in copper's morning upheaval.

# HYMN TO DAWN,
# HYMN TO DUSK

Scorched air, evaporating atmosphere,
pneumatic gash of sound sparrows
flash forward through
harnessed to the goddess's chariot
by a sash of woven flax threaded
with fine-spun copper
glinting with the light of the morning star.
                                    Plutonic
glacier of space, waxing
shine of the skin.
                    Untold tons
of volcanic ash the violence of birth uphurls.
Evaporation. Hellish destiny. No water. No rain.
Only a high-pressure blanket of
thick clouds and sulfuric acid driven
                                    by high winds
hot enough to melt lead. Orchestral
lumen of copper, brightening up a whole span

of the night sky, dawn
about to break.
                        Strong enough to cast
a shadow on Earth.


A splash of light
a shock of light
a texture of light
in night discerned
a copper flash
an orb in chains
a righteous intensity
a dragon at rest
a sword in hand
laughter in slaughter
furious revolution-
aries Venus
smiles on.


In the citadel of the sky
where the upsloping curve attains its
consummate form where the downsloping drop
makes its beginning and where the citadel of heaven
arises between dawn and dusk holding
the universe poised in its balance, here
the antique sons of Lucifer claim Venus alone
among the stars, announcing
with shock of light and copper flash

her radiant intensity
wherewith she rules the affairs of men.

You settle your eye onto

Saturn's eventual temple of Daemonium
built on the agitated edges of time.
Death's firm-bolted door Pluto occludes.
Mercury's moveable waystations glistening with linseed oil. These

pale next to Venus's
epochal volcanic flashes
a lusty squadron of Cytherean sparrows
enwreathe and energy's seismic alibis
inscribe.

Desire.

Venus's Satanic aspect
lashed like lightning and pouring evil
up into the world.

Temple towers in great basalt calderas

eruptive and destroying
any view to the tungol-punctured sky
beyond the menacing cloudhang—:

But there it is,

the splendor of Venus. The temptations

of her aureole. Lucifer
loose in late summer, sucking the cock
of Mars.

Oceanic Nemesis, burning with righteous anger,
daughter of the night, enemy of you who have violated the order of nature,
heaping up your trash under the diadem of her beauty.
Sixty-seven million miles from the Sun her scorn
radiates in the sky at night showing
these intensive forms of exploitation and degradation
you hope in Satanic shamelessness
to keep nevertheless from view. Nemesis. Black
as ink. Winged like a bat, like a
daemonic night flyer. Venus
in a moment of rage reshaped into Nemesis, head
adorned with a wreath of winged girls
attended by watchful
stags.

Desire.

Desire Venus intensifies.

Myrrha in prayer transformed her sins into a tree, plunging
her face into the bark that sheathed her, redolent
thereafter with royal scent she bore. Her
beautiful boy Venus herself adored.

From Cyprian Cinyras Myrrha was sister to Adonis her son. Desire's
forms annihilate even suicidal grief the scent of myrrh
exuded from a tree intoxicates. A magian gift
fit for a newborn lord.

Balsam
cinnamon
zedoary
flowers—:

myrrh is more enviable
than any of these.

Myrrh is the tree that weeps its fruit in spicy gums
and in the tusk of a boar is the flash of the lightning stroke.
Lions who reek with the slaughter of cattle.
Wolves who faint at the dark throb of the Moon sliding across the disc of
    the Sun
in midheaven, noon strobing down upon the world.

Nothing's velocity surpasses the year's.

Maculate shadowing of cloud work.
Agitated rustle of wind.
Even envy would praise his beauty. Adonis.

Desire.

Desire Venus intensifies.

Embowered in viburnum with Cupid cuddling—
he reaches up to kiss her cheek nicking with his arrow's tip
the supple curve of her breast—love's
sudden sore, rage
flashing by, and she pushes her beautiful son
away. The wound
goes deeper than she first felt and soon nothing—

not the outline of her island
not the breezeways of her palace
not the energetic forms of the sea from where she emerged
not the mineral wealth of all the Earth—

nothing
means more to her
than this man

        slicked in the fragrant resins
of his mother's arboreal tears, wrenched
from her womb of wood shaped
from the love for her father—his father—she bore
from which sin, now glorious in youth, her superb brother and son
was born.

      The boar.

Like a dream.

Tensing with Nemesis.

Flashed by the lad with a cunning spear to his ham.

Rooted out perfunctorily from the wound, shredded by its violence.

In a muscular surge, deep up into the groin,

sinking his rank tusks

and in that unwrenching laying out

the dying boy to gasp for life upon the yellow sand.

○

The love you feel is the light of the Sun
and its heat entrapped by volatile gasses terminally
changing the nature of the world you live in.
The goat-fish is a groundedness, the mean
between climbing and sinking.

The radiant mansion
is your visionary clock
begun in natal flush.

> *The gods*
> *lived in the souls*
>
> *of our ancestors*
> *and did not enter*
>
> *completely*
> *into any one story.*

But in this horoscope, you present some description of Heaven, the focus
of prayer, and the gate of hope. It is your nature,
assigned at your birth. You present your ruminations
on the planets, brilliant and sublime, and the angels
with their wings: twofold, threefold, and fourfold.
And on the stained hand of the stars
and on lightning flicked like the stroke of a bookkeeper's script
and on the vehement forms of passion
and on its torment. The sages

of Egypt are endocrines in your stream of thought and Venus
is a goddess of greeting and farewell. Just as the setting
of the evening star is the end of the world, so
the appearance of the morning star augurs
its beginning. The sciences
of Venus are vindictive, volcanic. The love
you're feeling is an agitation
in your nervous system from Venus rotating
slowly backwards from east to west—in love
a day is longer than a year.

You, tossed about on a darkening brim—.
You, withering in a deadly clasp.
You, feeling the traitorous touch, its tingle
on your heart.

You thane.
You thralled princeling.

You worker of magic the goddess of spume so
haughtily defies.

Heaven's genitals like cicadas at summer's end. Their
audacious rattle. The aerarium of the sea

they foam in. You witness in all the art and woe of civilization
her spectacular birth, fully formed and
curved with sex, from the brimming
mousse that flecks the surface of
the broth she
emerges from castrated storms
of light and wave riot over
thinned in time

to the murmuring of girls, the smiles of new
lovers, wiles and sweet delights, charm and bitterness
gusts of harm and need release to course
like rumors over the place in the sea
Venus.
Genetrix.

Veneration of Venus's dolorous attentions
vulcanizes
feeling
into passion
you summon impulsively, un-
certainly.

Luminous Venus heart of heaven
visible there on the cusp of dawn.
The temptations of her aureole—
offering her truant attentions
*the fire-eating steeds of the Sun*
are stunned by,
each day
a seduction
in
foam.

Venus's sparrows' helical pull of her chariot through emotional matter.
It's your self, washing in her life bothered
anew by her squadrons
of lusty finches.

Voluptuous Venus hero's mother nurturing goddess life's darling the Earth
bears forth every living thing for
and the brim of the sea
whisks all scum from and the light
of the Sun expands over in blushed dawn—she, goddess,
wind-fled, cloud-dashed, wonder-worked, she
of glittering skin in outpoured light—: she,
mounted on the writhing hump of antiquity's sea-ram
tugging on his beard for a rein and wreathed
by chains of sparrows sped forward by their lusts,
climbs through the gate of dawn and
with the point of consciousness punctures the heavens

so that her brilliant Vulcan influence streams
through your powers upon which she smiles
her ever-living charm.

Vespertine Venus, eophoric flame, rival of Sun and Moon, alone
among the stars shining with such brilliance
whose rays cast a shadow, auguring
the almighty Lord of the world:
Love.

Love dressed you in spangles, love
drew lines of beauty out of flesh, love pulled you
in by the vigors
of the *uterine clutch*.

About your neck you wore a circlet of silk, like a crown
in appearance, and you wore a ring of turquoise
diagonalized by strokes of silver lightning
around its band, Zuni
jewelry, not once removed since the moment
you met her, and you wore
the white gold and you burned
the sage. To Venus

are attributed raw aloe, musk, and the aromatic thistle
perfumers treasure; labdanum, mastic, threads of poppy, seed puffs of
milkweed, the bright orange buds of
Asclepius, and mace of the rattlesnake master. Each

of these is gathered in a mass and mixed with
rainwater collected in the buttercup's
summer chalice worked into a paste and squeezed
through a cloth. That day you

took the dew squeezed through a gauze of woven fibers and drew it up
into an eyedropper, depositing it in an apothecary's
vial. The past you expressed
you rolled into straws you
dried in the light of
the daystar.
                    Catching fire, the straws
fumed in a censer, a beautiful thing, an offering fit
for Love's prime tastes.
                                And then you summoned her, mistress
of good and gall, and she frightened you and
showed you her raptures, and wiving you she stroked
your needs and
holds you still
in her
thrall.

FROM THE SPECTACLE

OF YOUR IMAGINATION,

ITS EMANATING WAVES

The Sun's spasming laryngeal fountain
your birth in ways announced. Wreathes
of skylarks who stream from the sunlight's suffocating ecstasies.

# TOTALITY

Who beyond the corona's fuming magicum—in whose stunning
fury powers wreathe their forces—who
saw when you entered the Sun's stupefying throne room enameled
in saffron and horror
the fires in gold in ingoing undulation rebellow
into your nuclear self? Aroma
of myrrh the Holy Ghost groans in the abundant sense of.
Despondent roars that signal the curious
foreshapings of the spirit's

life. The Sun's foam. Its thrum
of force. The Sun's
theriomorphic lion. Eternity's
heliopolitan purr, its libidinal
boom
and pash.

It was not the Sun god you adored but the material
Sun itself which extending its hand of flame
touched you with an eternal life
belonging to the God in whom all things
are made.

The Sun's arrogant clasp.
The Sun's wrathless winter heat.

*The Sun*, you read, *is one foot wide*.

But what
could cover the Sun?

Rage.
Rage of gold in the temple of the Sun—
in the center of the earth where the Sun is black.

Dragons.
Migrating dragons in sun-wheeling pageants.

Shadow.
Shadow and gloom
from the Moon's sunward side. An early
afternoon's drifted-in dusk the Sun—
seething only crown—flares out
into the fixed stars' depths.

Wolves.
The wolves who faint at the death of the Sun.

○

The Sun's alchemy.
Specifically, the Sun's alchemical aridification.
The Sun's threat of desert.
The Sun's ecstasy of heat
and fermentation. Nature

keeps her secrets, loving to hide
the gush from two suns' collisions where gold
buried deep in the Earth's sinuses vibrates
with the powers of creation. You
will dig through tons of earth just
for an ounce of that gold,

a portion
of sunlight
to hide in
your pocket.

Creative murder of the risen Sun shining—
what God shall you adore with your oblation?
Earthmaker. In an aura
of unquiet fire. Him.
Him you worship weak
with awe.

The Sun's dwarven seeresses adorning his altars of light
with blood, a magma of gold

from violated earth
sacrificed in the name
of life.

It's a hideous scene
you've invented but turn your eyes from, ashamed
at your lust, its
intensities.

○

You have heard the Sun singing wildly, a corona of angels
expanding the chorus. And you have felt the Sun's power
streaming from within a living dynamolosis. And you have
stood in the Sun's chemical theater where you have seen
the Sun's horror of power the planets in circuits absorb.
And you have felt the Sun's ruthless hammer of gold. And stood
in the stupendous sun-clad ruins of the star
whose thatches of penumbra shade
cavities of plunging hydrogen
violent in agitation and size
angelic sun-gems arise from
purring with sundering powers of
revelation and holocaust.

○

Light itself
is always light
and illuminates the surrounding dark.

Aura of angelic powers whose foreheads marked
with the sign of the living God stream out from the rising Sun.

Whose holy powers are these?

To which you would answer: *God*

*is Power in that all power is contained within his own*
*self. God is power insofar as he*
*exceeds all power. God gives life to all things*
*through his power in the Sun which is total and*

*unthwarted.* The Sun's thundering havoc of heat
                                        and light.

The Sun's ancestral furies gushing their agonized bursts.
The Sun's uneven valves of gold
energy quakes through
                        sunbeams in torrents
gravity influng ravages
to enrapture the inner fringes of your self
on fire. Even

in constant aurora the Sun always gleams.
Pitch and nitre.
Abundant gunpowder.
Annihilating majesty.

The Sun
is an immortal strobe,
a sphere of flame
a throb
through void form
your mind ignites.

○

The older
the deity
the more terrifying
the god.
Worship
of the Sun
is worship
of the oldest
most
formidable
power—

witchcraft.
The Sun's energetic witchcraft.

In the throne room of the Sun, lioned with thundering gold, powers boom
and light forms pour out rings of fire.

In the solarium of the fall, lordly cranes winding up thermal gyres guide
loftiest currents to guttural calls fluted through their antique sinuses.

In the Sun's undone thrum of creation, heat and light outglory matter ebul-
lient angels bearing their messages seethe from.

In the swinging thurifer of the Sun, jets of the father's wrath.

In the soft delusion of eternity, the saffron silks of the Sun.

In the Sun's orbital quake, Elohim's coils of torture and euphoria.

In the annals of the black magic the stars nightly blind, the Sun's uneven
valves of gold.

In the dream of money flowing freely from one reliable source into your
cupped hands, the Sun's Satanic sieve, its hermaphroditic mesh.

In the Sun's brooding bulk, endless destruction and quenchless rage.

In the Sun's beguiling gold, chrysolite, carbuncle, myrrh, incense, moss,
amber, balsam, honey, aromatic reed, crocus, corn, aloes, cinnamon, and
loosestrife.

In the pour of the Waterman, the empowered Sun spasming in throes of
birth.


Earth of grains, earth of fat.

The Sun brightly shining. Its consummation.


The moist body of the heavens.

The blackness that results. The shadow.


○

The eclipsing Moon's deep-eyed arousal.

There is the Sun; the brass of light; the grove; the open field; the wolves of
    the Sun and von Hempel's dragons;
the morning, steaming. Deep in August. There, above, the Sun's sulfureous
    riot. Its
caustic fires. And there, invisible, the Moon, adrift, its
lenient salt. The cumbrous white cake of it. Approaching the Sun's
white magnesium. Terraqueous men. Everywhere. Salamandrine
men and women assembled. Children of the Moon
in the throbbing heat. Wearing pitchy spectacles. Delicately
extracting snacks from boxes and bags. What
land of darkness in vibrant morning light alluded to. What land
of darkness to be brightened by a polarized gloam. What land of
solar quakes and escharotic eruptions.
What skin of a burn on the world.
What Satanic void arriving.

Thin Sun, new Moon incurring.
Intensely polarized light, like looking through crystalized shadow.
Lunulae of light pass through pinhole apertures of leaves
feathering the surface of things with their small silver
scythes.

Nemesis Moon.
Sun's acetylene sliver.
A minute before total eclipse, the Sun's
intense fuse little more than a crescent

like the sting from a welder's torch swung
in an outlining arch. Stars

and planets.
Jupiter first, benignant herald.
A hush—insects settling down.

Totality.
Gasps of awe incanted
in euphoric disbelief. For
two minutes and seventeen seconds
where the Sun was there is instead a great opaque throb
surrounded in brilliant silver, the Sun's
superheated atmospheric corona
like a great radiant exhalation. The Sun
every hour leaking
seven billion tons of corona
into space the solar winds
suspire from. You

can't stop looking at it. Like

beholding the eye of God—for a moment, a reprieve,
until God unwinks and restores Eternity.

To stare at the Sun!
Pleas of disoriented unbound joy.
And the wolves have all fainted.

And the Moon's soporific witchcraft absorbs the Sun's
subliming heaves.

And the brass is clashed among the peoples of the Middle West
whose cymbals urge the magicians' incantations, the ones
drawing down the Moon from the heavens.
And the staggering boy clutching his temples whose migraine
the eclipse has triggered.
And the eclipsed Sun's meteoric moonshine.
Its glossy Babylonian veneer. The Sun! A dark throbbing socket of terror
whose silver corona intones
transplendent starlight
unfringed

in the eclipsing Moon's
deep-eyed arousal.

○

You

must conceive of the shape of the body
that encloses all things as circular, for such
is the shape of the universe. An eclipse

is the descent of the Sun into the Fountain of Mercury.
The Sun in the embrace of the dark Moon is treacherously
slain by the snakebite of the mother-beloved.

A virgin with a serpent's tail
typically complicit with the transmission of knowledge.

A calf is born with two heads and five legs.
A cock has laid an egg.
An old woman has a dream of border crossing.
(A second language is spoken, convincingly.)
A comet appears in the sky.
There is a raging fire in the town nearby.
And the following year, at the hands of a demented leader,
war breaks out.

The law of duplication.
The law of totality.
The sorcerer's omen.
The Sun's disturbing glossaries.
The Sun's distorted glossolalia.

And the inhabitants of the Earth wailing to be created.

○

Sun gushing agonized light through the valves of life.
Flaming wheel upheld before your torso.
Five-pointed immensus of the Sun.
Sun whose fiery doors were closed.

Angels in the silver streaming from the blind spot of the Sun.

Sulfureous stones of the Sun lodged
in the crypts of the sky's tonsils. Eclipse's
woven shadow. Angels
weaving from feeling
a mesh in the throat of your birth. An
esophageal web of the Sun.

Go ahead. Try it.
To swallow all the soreness you've
inherited. You can't.
All these seething suns. You can't do it. You'll
have to live instead. In the light
of the Sun that the Moon attends,

your imminent psychic birth transpends.

You balance on cymbals percussing the sea. You offer
wings of fire to the Sun and
unloosed winds to the Moon. The lions

of noon have swallowed the Sun
revealing the mystery kept secret for aeons
from eternity's tacit thrumming of time
the Moon's dark side
harrows in umbra at midday. It's this:

You can't swallow the Sun yourself.
Despite the quicksilver meteors you keep in your pockets,

despite the aura of transmutation as your thoughts
from feelings sublime, despite
Jovial benisons choired down from on high, the Sun
is something you can't
swallow yourself. Only

in the Moon's magnificent mirk
can you do it, can you
swallow the fire
gushing from the Sun's silvering
fountain

to know

that it's the outer and not the inner life
that the stars from the time of your birth have been showing you
but that you've failed to see
all these years
with the Sun ablaze
in the sky overhead until
totality's moment of dazzle, when the Moon
drifted for two minutes across the eye of life, and you saw
all of it, the awe of it. There is

no life in the Sun without
forgiveness, especially of
Father Sun himself.

FROM THE SPECTACLE

OF YOUR IMAGINATION,

ITS WRATH


You would slaughter all the oceanic stars
to boast about doing so.

# THE BLADE

Blind. Raging. Furibund.
Feral. Wild. Untamable. Overpowering. Excessive.
*Insanus*. Bloody. Sclerotic. Profaned
by crime. Swift. Sudden.
Atrocious. Horrible. Vehement.
Lascivious. Unrestrained. Cock-combed.
Spear-carrying. Turpid. Aspered. Foul, loathsome, obscene, disgraceful.
Rough, bristling, shaggy.
Disordered. Confused. Unarticulated.
Savage. Harsh. Archaic. Ancient.

Slayer of men.
Destroyer of worlds.
Murderer. Fatal
to mortals. Kraterion. Brutally,
supernaturally powerful.
Audacious. Rabid. The battle rage
that is life's force.
Victims.
In gruesome numbers.

Mars's massive arsenal of terror.
Mars's hollow art of brinkmanship.
Mars's push from the blade to the gun. Strife's
thralldom Mars strokes. You speak about, you speak to Mars in his own style.

Mars's pneumatic throne of glass—the whole
draconic economy of Satan that
shatters it. War's

melancholic handclasp, its
wasps' nest of apocalypse. War's warp. War's
discord, dissonance, shock. War's rupture, schism,
rifts, feuds. War's brawl. War's row. War's
racket. War's riot.

The gun. The sword. The death. The knife.
Mars's demiurgical blade
you marvel at, having received its avatar
as a gift.

The small precious objects of Mars. The rapt awe
you hold them in, radiant
with strife, balanced in the hand, ready
to strike.

Mars with his haughty disdain. Mars
with his shining helmet, with his polished bronze.
Mars with his gun in hand and cheap bullets in his pockets.

Mars shitting on life, on the living. Mars sullenly defending his ground
at the back of the train car. "Don't stand near me. Stand
over there." Mars riding his chariot of iron
around the flaming Sun. Mars
constantly succumbing to appetite—
lusts and rages, swarms of violence and
seething angers he coaxes from you as you
walk through the city spoiling
to kick somebody's ass.

Trusted barbed bombast of Mars's enviable blade.
As good for war as for surgical grief.
Or chopping the onion that causes you to weep.

Rypophagous world rotating below the heavenly sheen where Mars,
heaving garbage, urges your quarrels
with friends to explode. Volcanic
passions enacted as battles. War
is the father, the king, and the master.

The serpent sacred to Mars with its wondrous golden crest—
its eyes flashing fire, the venom
gorging its length, the ominous flicking in and out
of its tongue with its three-pronged
fork. And its teeth in three sharp rows like
the fangs of a she-wolf sheathed
in sin.

          The serpent
sacred to Mars the weary Tyrian wayfarers looking for a spring to drink from
     startle
from slumber deep in a troglodytic silence—in horror
they drop their urns. They are seized
with fear. And the serpent as suddenly undular as a
lamprey unwrithes from braided coils
to tilt into a martial bow as huge
in the otherwise untremoring air
as Draco's never-hidden circumpolar length outstretched
between the bears
who maul the stars. With lashing fangs, with
crushing throbs, with poisoned force—all of Cadmus's men
are slain.

          The serpent
sacred to Mars whom Cadmus favored by Athena seething with vengeance
in turn will slay.

What sibilant hiss, what mysterious coiling in the zodiac uplifted
whose deadly magics drive
Mars's malevolent fuckerei. These

rough
martial combats.

Go pour out your wrath from the vial of bloody sunlight you carry as your
     charm.

Go say to the victims of rapture and rape and waste from our days, "It is done."
Go prepare the way for war and the rumor of war.
Go show them war's irruptions as revelation and
outbreak.

The blade and the storm. The feel and the wreckage. The huge
arrowing agonies.

> Armies on the move across the plains, the wastes.
> What are you burning? What
> are you sacrificing? And what are you doing
> with that blade?

> > *The sorcery of nature.*
> > *The noiseless road.*
> > *The elusive law.*

The blade that Mars would yield
Mercury clasps, running his slender fingers tenderly
along the smooth curves
of its walnut handle. Though Mars
wants it
Mercury made this blade from an elevator cable
and not on a forge but in the fires
of the mind.

Is a pencil an unnerving
blade? And which are the nerves frayed by the scalpel

held in the surgeon's exacting hand?
What are the collections violence
obliges? And what are the virtues of
carrying a weapon? Whose hand wraps fitfully
around the hilt of helplessness? When
does iron shaped into a blade
do its greatest damage? Who guides the hand
that plunges the blade of stone into the trenches
of the earth? What ecstasies of onslaught, what
defiances of courtesy await you
in the orgying rapture
a faith in the world impels? Who
is the solicitor of all these ruinous
agonies? Whose ferrous storm
warms in the aura of life?

What is the form of harm
the blade you hold would
arm you from?

They say that Mars can sometimes imitate the Sun
in some of his gifts, radiating
a golden glory, but you know
martial things are a poison to the animal spirit
whose daemonic forays shun
what the Arab astrologers would call
"influences most baleful."

Mars's scorching flames match Saturn's native ice.

There are
Mars's two-hour twilights and there is the wounding
of Mars. An act all the chronicles narrate.


There is Diomedes with his spear. With Athena pressing the shaft—she
strengthens the thrust. Revolution-
aries writhe in combat around them. There is Mars in fancy
battle regalia and the thrust of the mortal spear
up then into his gut. Lurid pain. And then
there is Mars bellowing like a fighter jet
tearing a sudden patch from the sound barrier. Not one but
ten thousand fighter jets at once. So that
earth and air rebellow the roar
in suspended seconds after. Clouds. Leprous
with the brooding plague of darkness. And thunder. There
is Mars. Wincing in agony tears
that stain his grimace. As when
the cyclone hulled of anticipation unnerves the storm that bore it
coiling murky darkness shunned wonder in horror
shines on, so does bright Mars
grievously wounded with injury and shame,
flush with blood and sulking in woe, fly up at last to heaven
where he belongs.

FROM THE SPECTACLE

OF YOUR IMAGINATION,

ITS BROADMINDEDNESS

A darkening ceiling of hammered tin you lord under dabbing
with whitewash the stars
a virginal orderliness shines with.

# THE SECRET STRENGTH

# OF THINGS

*which governs all thought*

SEVEN IMAGES OF JUPITER

"an undisciplined overflowing of the soul"

FIRST IMAGE
*The Dream*

You awaken from the dream which was teeming with scolds whose
story smokes dayward in the random undazzling
of sleep's end to hear the jovial command urging:
*You will found*
*an institute*
*for the advancement*
*of the sacro-magical sciences. Not*
*in my name but surely*
*for my pleasure.*

○

Because Jupiter domineers, you
dream of kingdoms, of magistracies, of hours

and especially
of institutes of esoteric pursuits.

> *There be Jovial and Saturnine inhabitants*
> *as Galileo hath evinced already by his glasses.*

○

Jupiter who weighs destinies.

○

Jove's vastness alone rouses
a sense of pleasure drawn along
gravities' inevitable
adhesions.

○

Jupiter's usurpation of melancholy Saturn's rule.
Who sluices through Zeus's laws?
Jupiter's fortunes, Jupiter's mysterious ribboning bands.

Jupiter's complex spectroscopy, sunlight
of different wavelengths absorbed at various
depths within the atmosphere's bright bands of

cloud down to
staggering
depths.

Jupiter's radiogenic heat. *Jupiter*
*is so massive it could still be leaking out*
*a significant amount*
*of primordial heat trapped within*
*since its formation.*

Cloudtops are roiled ribbons of Jupiter's outer circumference.

At Jupiter's core, an envelope of hydrogen in excess of three hundred Earth
    masses and
*a sea of hydrogen that behaves like molten metal.*

Jove's interwoven simplex, Jove's
interdrawn
lunium. Jupiter's

music in the Lydian mode sounding
embryonic Jupiter's gravitational sway
over the formation of the other
planets in the young
cosmos.

    You
awaken from your dream to find
one stunning image of Jupiter after another

flashed forth from Juno's vigilant telegraphy, more
color and awe than are fair.

Yours is a Jovial institute, formed
to catalogue these powers and convey their
esoteric grandeur. You are bidding farewell
to that light sitting in the west to turn
to salute the new light rising in the radial east.

SECOND IMAGE

*The Facts*

Jupiter's magnificent *Quellgeist*, the gentle source of life.
And Juno's glimpses of Jupiter's magnificence—
Jupiter's auroral robe of cloud,
      peacock's eyes in hurricane stares—
Nothing else like Jupiter in the heavens.

                          These
orbic surges of storm eyes vortical irises glare from and
ribbons in bands of finery regally furl from.

Jupiter's atmosphere of molecular hydrogen and helium
many thousands of miles thick. Jupiter
the solar system's fastest rotator, its
hydrogen and helium very close to its
primordial composition—
                    methane and ammonia

color the atmosphere
red, brown, yellow, blue—.

Its faint ring captured
by Voyager in
sunlight. Jupiter's

composition the same as that of a star, its
ethereal nature—no
real difference between its atmosphere and its
denser layers. Jupiter's
dominance of the solar system, its mass
two-and-a-half times greater than all of the other
planets in the system
combined.

IVPETER DOMINVS

Only the Sun's gravitational field surpasses Jupiter's.

And the Jovian moons, discovered by Galileo in 1610 unequivocally
    transforming
the divine symmetry of an Earth-centered cosmos:

                    Callisto   Ganymede   Europa   Io

"sister worlds"                    mythically named

                    Astrologers initially
          calculated their motions
                              into emerging horoscopes.


Io's elliptical orbit that squeezes the moon
like a planetary fruit
causing a friction
that produces continuous seething heat and
endless volcanic eruptions, plumes of rock behaving
like boiling water
geysering hundreds of miles above its surface in
spectacular frosty displays.




                    THIRD IMAGE
                       *Myth*


Saturn
gone to the world of death, the world
          of the living drawn instead in Jove's way, the silver age and its
     argenteous race, dulled
as hammered tin, came in, worse
               than gold but
                    better than yellow
                         brass. Jove then bound time,
          shortening an everlasting spring with
     brumal surges the people suffered through, wary of

   fiercest

       ice and wind—


   until Jove forced down the Sun and
  *the parched air glared white with burning heat*: summer and
winter in silverine extremities. Rather


  than care or dense
  thickets


  the people built houses, made
  lasting shelters,
  sewed seeds, dug
  furrows


 and the oxen pulling the plows groaned under
    the weight of the yoke of the age
of Jupiter—lord of the sky in his tower
     of fire.


FOURTH IMAGE
*Destiny*


How do you tell the Sun from the god
whose strobes acquire the vortexes? The Sun
is your emanating source,
but there's a king who strides

the paths of ether
to light the futures depicted there
who strums the light like strings on a lute and whose
luteous robes are swirled with
atmospheric billows of ochreous saffron and
lurid blue in vibrant storms exchanging
color for cosmic vision. Jupiter. Chronocratic lord of benevolence and law.
*Iupiter Lucelius* and *Iupiter Fulgorator*. Magical empowerer who loves most
    the oak
as the tree his lighting most often strikes.

The whole nature of the sky is inexhaustible
hierophany. Everything that happens in the upper reaches or
among the stars—the rhythmic
revolution of the stars, chasing clouds, storms,
thunderbolts, meteors, rainbows—each thing
is a band of light in that
flashing manifestation. Jupiter's

punishing drunken joy, a prophetic
excitation of weather and magical teachings
hurricanes and rain

fertilize with vision—Jupiter's storms
are a supreme unleashing of creative force. Could the ancients, could
even Galileo have foreseen that Jupiter
would rotate and roil so rapidly with
storms incessant in constant

vastagonal showings
that only confirm his
irrefutable celestial magnificence?

It's
Jupiter's attainment of self-directed picture
consciousness.
Pantocratic Jupiter presaging the Lord enthroned in glory.
Bees

with tremoring abdomens clasping a honeycomb from whose golden dew
Melissa,
priestess of the bees,
fed the infant Zeus. Jupiter
is the thorax of a great transformation.

Jupiter foredreams Christ on high
amid heavenly powers a synaxis of angels cluster under
encombing an energy of God.

Presiding over the destinies of the world.

And what's your destiny. That word
that thrums with glory an alluring aura
that draws you towards its spectacular promise
even four-and-a-third of
Jupiter's grand revolutions resists

any faithful understandings of.

A scintillating nimbus. In whose patina a promise
for foreknowledge flashes with quicksilver
intensity. Your destiny

is unclear
but your ethos
tells you the time has come for the founding
of your own
temple of the law, this

Institute for the Advancement of the Sacro-Magical Sciences

whose name and founding
were spoken to you in a dream.

You in whom
time
would thrum
its hymn.

You
in whom the image is vortical.
In whom the image is vastagonal.
Under whom the pewter throne like a great celestial uplift
rests.

*Magic Powers*

As the true cosmic sovereign that he is, Jupiter
intervenes in history not like Mars
by physical or military force but
by his magical powers.

○

Jupiter's absence of axial seasons.
Jupiter's spirit of intelligence.
Jupiter's travel through the sixth sphere every
twelve years. Jove's
beard—a silver-leaved woodblade. Jupiter's
tin, Jupiter's topaz, Jupiter's
left ear.

*Song of Jupiter Prophetic*

| | |
|---|---|
| You are an eye of towering cloud | for amplitude |
| You are a storm surge's wave form | for bright terrible power |
| You are the sound of the love of life | for *Quellgeist* |
| You are a stag of thicketed tines | for awe |
| You are a raptorial spirit bird | for rapine lusts |
| You are the cloud-assembling downpourer. | |

You are the biblical dweller, having more to do with the depths than the sky.
You are the serpent-formed god who can be appeased with honey

all for literary power

You are the fungal lung and the natural spirit.
You are the wind
and you are what stirs the seas                    for meteorites

You are the esoteric core

*Fortuna*

You are Nemesis's lusty pursuer.
You were taken away to the upper reaches of swelling cloud forms
at the edge of the world by
the magical power of heaven—

only
then were you known by it, only then
was it really thrown into you
by the gentle source of life.

By this hypaethral immersion, from
this atmospheric volutation you
thrilled through, you've
gained powers of life—unsurpassable
pleasures in institutions and
academies of the trochilic
furl and the esoteric knurl.

*Visions of Juno, Forces of Storm*

Jovian tempests whose storms surging every twelve years
bring furor and triumph
the heavens roil with in unsmoothed and
rippling flows. *A Jovian tumult,*

the sages recorded, *remains*
*a tumult.*

Commotive and uproaring
glorying higher where the midheaven spikes
into a shining watchlight
whose potencies claim
authority magic commands in the zodiac's great
spinning allure.

○

"High above the Jovian clouds" is Juno in arching
circulations, her camera trained on the seething
surface of Jupiter's colossal and storming
atmosphere to see:

Jupiter's labial creams
Jupiter's turbulent shog, a fume of eyes—
Jupiter's gyrostatic wallows, his

blue eddying furls
of unruly depths and contours. You

don't need to know anything about the Jovian tempests'
enwrapping dimensions of teal curling into sable—

labia like fungal jelly—

to feel that this is the greatest thing to see
in all the heavens, this shapeshifting rage of gasses and
light, greater than any
orbital resonance or
plunge of gravity, greater even
than the Sun's spectacular suicide in flame—no:

the unspun dustswarm's ribbon Jupiter's circumferential storms band and
    surge through
is greater;
this planetary heavenwolken of Venetian endpapers Jupiter's colossal tropo-
    sphere encloses
is greater;
the cloud-top gravity defying its core's staggering atmospheric pressure,
    enough for solids and liquids to behave in unison
to engender this vision
is greater;
Jupiter's excessively vortical sky forms in creams and plumes in vastitude
    ramify, permutating swirls in an ongoing unrelenting act

is greater;

its labial poutings of cloud, its hurricane eyes, its visionary focus, its hiero-
    magian invocations of gas and light

are greater—


        Jupiter

of the fury, of the storms,

of the demon, of the convulsion,

of the sulfureous blues,

of the helial ochres,

of the dissilience and the squall,

of the voice and the command


whose hallways newly polished by the wingstrokes of a thousand

migrating songbirds reflect

the intentions and ideals of

the sacro-magical sciences and their advancement.



SEVENTH IMAGE

*Return to the Dream*


The white Sun's sudden aspect of extraordinary pallor.

A pale white western horizon. Dread.

And pallor. To stress the pallor of the orb's

terrifying vastness.

        A second sun's

distinctive form. A sphere and not
a disk, the shape of the now-setting Sun. The second sun
sliding more completely into
view.
    Strength
and majesty of the new sun in
the darkening sky. Fear
unformed by new awe.
                Jupiter
drifting closer to the Earth because of
extraordinary happenings going on all around.
                                 One

Jupiter yields to seven. These Jupiters
cruise into view forming
a planetary diadem.


                        ○


Jupiter's shepherding jeopardy pendulous lilacs drooping
with rainfall defy—your seat
is set

at Pythagoras's onomantic table—: It is time,
with the blessings of Jove,
                 to convene
the council of the hierologers and to begin
to divine the sacred names of things.
                         Spring's

mercurial floral gash of scents a garland
of lilac and viburnum crowns you with vernal law
as you enter this new psychic
institution the temple of the Earth
will shelter as long as this epoch

lasts.

# FROM THE SPECTACLE
## OF YOUR IMAGINATION,
### ITS RESTRICTIONS

On a leaden throne, a sullen, churlish, careful, always silent
Lord of Time flicks a sparking lighter the Moon's cool blue enlumes.

# THE SORCERER OF TIME

What brings you into communion with the sidereal gods? Is there
some foretaste of that bliss in store for you
upon the death of your soul? Your doctrines of immortality
are incomplete.

       Saturn's

melancholy boon is the magic
of life after death—he
oversees those sublime zones
of dread.

      Consider:

Saturn's magnetic influence
Saturn's maleficent intent
Saturn's concentric sorceries
Saturn's preponderance, sway, and pull
Saturn's regnancy, Saturn's resigned circumlocutions of time, Saturn's
    remote hegemony, Saturn's background dominance
Saturn's colossal retroaction

Saturn's command of space, extension, range, expanse, stretch, capacity,
   room, accommodation, scope, latitude, field, way, expansion, compass,
   sweep, spread
Saturn's vitreated night umber
Saturn's necklaces of meteoric ice and nebular smoke.


To call upon Saturn it is necessary
for you to await a favorable moment, to wear
black vestments, to approach the sacred place in
meditative gloom, sunk in sorrow, to burn a perfume
composed of incense and opium mixed
with grease and the urine of a goat and then
at the moment the smoke arises, to raise your eyes to the stars.


Saturn: Cold and dry. Male. Diurnal. Disagreeable and astringent. Offensively
   acidic. Stinking. Jet black and black mixed with yellow. Lead in color.
Saturn: A pitch-black throne.
Saturn: First climate and barren mountain. Wednesday night and Saturday
   night.
Saturn: Underground canals and vaults. Wells, old buildings, desolate roads,
   lairs of wild beasts, deserts full of them, stables for horses, asses, camels,
   and elephants. Equatorial zones. The rumor of night the day spreads out
   from noon.
Saturn: Litharge, iron slag, hard stones. Lead. Pepper, beleric myrobalan,
   olives, medlars, bitter pomegranate, lentils, linseed, hempseed.
Saturn: Drugs cold and dry in the fourth degree, especially those which are
   narcotic and poisonous. Dwellings. Sleep. Retentive power.

Saturn: Fleas, scorpions, snakes, beetles. Goats. Fatigue. Absence of hymns. (No real tradition of praise.)

Saturn: The element of earth. The condition of lead. The angelism of thrones. Ravens. Swallows. Flies. Black bile and crude phlegm. Hair, nails, skin, feathers, wool, bones, marrow, and horn. Spleen.

Saturn: Strengthening and forging through tension and resistance.

Saturn: Sickness, affliction, poverty, death, disease of internal organs, gout. Those who own estates. Kings' attendants. Religious seekers of various sects, priests especially. Those whose discipline compels them to write things down in notebooks daily. Devotees, wicked people, bores, the overworked, eunuchs, thieves, the moribund, magicians, demons, ghouls, those who revile them.

Saturn: Water, ammonia, methane. Rings of ice. From glacial blocks to minute particles. A zone of electrically conducting fluid undergoing convective motion. A pressure greater than two million atmospheres. Hydrogen electrons no longer confined to atoms, flowing through a sea of hydrogen that behaves like a molten metal.

Saturn: Convective motion, impenetrable magnetosphere. Rings and moons. Ice reflecting sunlight intensely where the rings are mostly densely packed. Enceledus's terrific venting of ice crystals, replenishing the rings.

Titan: Cryovolcanic dynamism. Its branching channels methane pours through.

Titan: Photochemical derivatives that turn it into an opaque smog.

Titan: Lithosphere decoupled from the interior by a planet-scale internal ocean. Windblown dunes of ice. Lakes of methane with marshy fringes. Methane rainfall. Dendritic drainage channels feeding the methane lakes.

Saturn's rings: One of the heaven's most glorious features.

Hymns to Saturn are sparse. Saturn's
melancholy magicum. At this moment, out of its gloom,
spurred by moonlight, the leaden material of your soul
is born.

        Consumed by worries solicited from senseless truths and
pointless spending—desires wire you
for woe. But why? You waste
your life pursuing
phantom gains—material pleasure, a wish for widespread
recognition—time
tediously evaporates. You're poorer for your possessions,
including your ambitions, because your desire
leaves you always wanting more. Luxuries
purchased dispossessing fear ruins—what you have you'll
surely lose.

        Saturn's limiting
and regal disdain. Saturn's compositional majesty. Saturn's
slow burn. The chronism of Saturn's Satanic
thistle. Saturn's draconian
plasmas, its elegant
orbiting rings consisting of
stellar debris and theophany.

        Take heart, you fool. Fate
rules this world, the next world, and all the orbiting lords
of heaven, and all the dimensions and all the dust—whose
laws fix all things and all the long ages
which time signs with destiny.

        Another, greater

power rules than you can imagine, keeping you
from a leaden throne cuttlefish
in intelligent squadrons have stained with ink
the black biles of melancholy invidiously coat.

Need

you be told again of the Roman heresiarch who rescued
the vestal fire from the flames ravaging the temple of the city? You're
no Roman here but the temple itself that time
consumes in cool, sad, decreasing
rings.

*Who obtains astral immortality? How does*
*the soul ascend to heaven? Where is the abode of the blest*
*to be found? What blessings or sorceries vouchsafe*
*your access to this ascension?*

The transience

of Saturn's slow-turning exhalations, his lugubrious
auguring realities.


Saturn said:
"Wait! I have eaten all the books
of all the learning of all the arts from all the islands
and inhabited places unlocking
all the lore-craft and knowledge of magic
the Libyans and Pythagoreans have hidden in sciences
disciples of lore carry in memory. Soothsayers
have guided me to discipline's wisdom
in many a mighty book
I've devoured and swallowed on the edge of a sword . . .

Such knowledges could I have joined together not even
in all the ancient scriptures. Fate. Fate's
defiant telepathies, fate's theurgical
witcheries, fate's planetary clairvoyances—these
have been my summons. Time
curls them into rings visible
through a telescope.
                    I sought nevertheless
which moods, which majesties, which
zeals and riches, which
ranger's virtues and cunning
were there for me
in the pine-rioting northern forests'
prayer to the creator.
                    All of it entirely I'll
give you in tribute, son of the resurrection,
burning whelm and wave and fire, thirty pounds
alchemical gold and my children too—Jupiter, Neptune, Pluto, Juno, Ceres,
    and Vesta—
if you bring me to the edge of that total urge
Christ's canticle's homily incites truth in,
and I'll leave here sound in purpose in good will
wending myself onward along the water's ridge
over the river Chobar to seek the Chaldeans
whose magic's craftwork is soothsaid and foretold
in the planetary motions and the future whose scent
their movement emits."

Saturn said:

"But who most
of all creatures of destiny
can open the holy doors to the kingdom of heaven
to reveal that radiance readied by
hardships formed in ancient
agitations and magic?"

Saturn said:

"No one knows,
no hero, no firmamental savior, how my mind weakens
busy after books—sometimes in me a great burning rises up
near soul's desire seething there utterly
anxious and afire."

Saturn said:

"Bold is the one who feasts on the crafts of books—
who holds this power will always be wiser."

○

You have passed through the portal of toil into
a night of melancholy gloom—as the world cools, you
dry, all the moisture of your vitality
evaporating from you. Doom comes
feeling like
a need for sleep fitfully but wearily
resisted until

it feels there is no other choice but
like Saturn to descend into the labyrinthine crypts
of sleep whose empty casks of vital liquors are slicked
inside with a film of death, residue
from the creation itself where Saturn
reigned as the first great Lord of Time. Look. Now
he's so feeble, a refugee from his own
chronocracy time has eroded the grand architectures of
keystone by keystone. Satanic cowards, vicious
in their destructive glee, flash
their fangs and devour their young,
everyone cheering on while Tartarian Saturn
draws down the least visible sustenance from the milk
of death, easing annually deeper into the deepest vault of
sleep, powerless to draw even the lightest limits
on the politicians' free-for-all frolic with
corruptions they'd as soon rape as seduce.
Saturn's shadow oozing outward uncontrolled.
"And Hell is the realm of God's self-loathing," is what the poet
wrote a half-century ago.

○

          Saturn's
Neoplatonic marathon, its melancholy lodestone
the Renaissance endowed in Ficino's lavish obsession
with transformative fright
and grace.

      Saturn's mirroring
of the origins of the solar system in its vast
curl.
      Saturn's thirty-year orbit (two and change in
most lifetimes) and ten-and-a-half hour
rotation.
      Saturn's rings reflecting the vanished solar disc
from which creation itself occurred. Each ring's
immense speed and endless collisions of ice particles.
                                       Saturn's
sixty-two moons: Dione, tidally locked to the planet; Iapetus
with its equatorial ring half in ice, half in black dust; Titan—
larger than Mercury with its fully developed atmosphere;
Enceledus, the most reflective object in the solar system mirroring
*all* the sunlight that strikes it—giant fountains of ice
geysering out of its geothermic tiger stripes; these moons'
magnificent desolation.

Saturn's slow
sad turn.

Saturn's long-form melancholy
in the scattered shadow of the sudden light of resurrection.

Saturn's circumstantial friendship with the Moon, your Moon
with its daring sliver, that your mother in the gesture of birth
like a paper lantern set
aloft in the night air where

Saturn, alongside, has been brooding
all your life.
              Melancholic surges
of a global hidden ocean in Saturn's
lunar life, shaper and destroyer of time—.

                    ○

The controlling hands' powdered ochres; cavernous
shadows it's emerging from—
                           the sensitivity suggested
by Saturn's outstretched hand, the supplication to
even older cosmic powers, invisible
to all but coeval
epiphanies.
              A cave bear's antique
clawings.
              Saturn's hand
considered the giver of life and of strength. Long-vanished
prehistoric memories the gesture
of the outstretched hand suggests, that the seeds
of the life-soul came out of his fingernails.

The Saturnine orb's
warped vision, its medieval
Phrygian
modes—

Saturn's aerarium, its
Tables of the Law
kept there.

Saturn's lyrical rhapsody for the falling age.
Saturn's epochal exacerbations, his
long-drawn, heavy-lidded
resignation and
devastating
limitations.

Saturn's festival of death in the old saeculum.
Saturn devouring all his sons and daughters.
Saturn as Kronos devouring all his daughters and sons.
The insufferable grief of Saturn as Kronos devouring all his daughters and
    sons—.
Saturn the archaic and tortured thinker.
There's the great stone in swaddling clothes given to the son of the sky who
    seized the stone and thrust it into his stomach.
In an ancient golden age, honey flowed from the oaks.
Saturn and the Golden Age exist even still in the outermost edge of things.
Saturn sealed in a sphere of lead
encompassed three times by the walls of night.

You're aware, only incrementally, of its vast
cycle moving so slow, it's nearly as
invisible as it is restrictive. Also its sorcery.

And its great beauty.
                              You've tried for years to expand with
each area in your life responding
to the effort. But astromancy unsays its
spells even as they're uttered and Saturn—brooding through
his long curl—gathers the shattered pieces of
your broken incantations. You're limited, pilgrim. You'll
never become secure in your profession. That's a limit. You'll never
win wide acclaim. That's a limit. You'll never stop
working to earn your keep. That's a limit. You've never unlink your emotional
    life
from the troubles in your home as a child. That's another limit. You'll
never serve any power but Mercury in your interests and
pursuits. That's a kind of limit. You'll never
be free of sin. That's a law of life. But even in Saturn's
malefic resignation, vibrating in harmony with celestial
music, the Lord of Lead and life's chronocrat
offers to you a defining gift:
                                    *discipline*.


                                    However
long it takes you, cultivate its benefits and
marry them to the Moon, moist and changeable
and cruising attractively
in an arc
across
the night sky.

The Sun is God. Mercury angelic forms. The Moon
your soul. And Saturn? Magic's
primordial daemonism—

the archaic sorcery that sets
the schema spinning.

FROM THE SPECTACLE

OF YOUR IMAGINATION,

ITS RADICAL PERTURBATIONS


A cherub flares in midheaven in the House of the Father,
a gravitational quirk spiked with virginal fizz.

# AT THE GATES OF DELIRIUM

*What is music?*
*What is poetry?*
*What is mythology?*

The Uranian secret is Promethean,
                              revolutionary.
How was this secret transmitted to you? Simple:
you asked to be a poet. And how did it feel?
Fulgurating, starry, accelerated, interior, like
the invention of a technology for terror but used
in an act of kindness, a terroir
of a force field's alien magic you'd learned
at the knees of a master after years of
petition.
          What master?

You met him at the bottom of a staircase, wreathed in fumes
of Marlboro Lights, an aura of antique authority
enlivening him. He led you up
into the shadows of Elgin Park

where the poetry
was laid out like energetic, architectonic
tiles in multiple
                    dimensions, each an absorber and
magnifier of attention: Look—images. Images
everywhere. And leading you through them: a master
of the faculty by which images, actual and poetic, are
understood.
              A cat would purr in his lap. Modernism
arranged itself in his living room—
                              tubular
Bauhaus chairs, shelves crammed with dogeared
volumes of poetry, holograph books filled
with the signatures of a who's who of poets and
artists from the thriving mid-century—


                              Prometheus,
bristling with energy in his revealed body,
                              heaved
your old life out the window
where it slumped at the base of the huge pharaonic columns
supporting the expressway the cars
in unending streams
flowed over.

You were twenty-four.

Your new life? You
summoned it in correspondences, the principle
of magic and exchange—poems

passed from hand to hand by word, neatly typed
and folded carefully into envelopes. As radically simple and
revolutionary as a thing can be.
                        And what did you learn?

Everything.

You marveled at the crafts and resources contrived by rebellion—learning
among them the greatest: Leechcraft and herbcraft with leechwort
and ointment, omen and oil. Balsamic bindings, words
with power. Seercraft
you learned, ominous
dread, visions from sleep, rest's agitations—hard
to interpret but exchange is the key. Birds. Flocking
and solitary, their auspices and mysteries. Worlds they inhabit,
this one and the next. Looking at entrails is
something else you learned, the way winding around a
sacred truth their smoothness glistens auguring
pleasures divine powers take in *the dappled beauty of the gall and the lobe*.
You learned to take thighs wrapped in unctuous tallow
and burn them on the sacrificial altars
of chalk, and how mortals, involuntary, plod always
to the base of that violet table. You learned

the flaming signs of the sky in gloomier times so dim.
You learned the aspect and the transit, all the melancholy
houses, the eminence and the intermediaries, the seasons and
the sidereal gods, the vault and the myth,
the sublunary daemonism imbuing the silver-blue light
with texture and shadow. How do you know
any of these things are true?


*Feeling.*


How?


The eophanic visionary reality of the dawn world
beamed into this world through feeling.

What can be seen in
other worlds through seercraft or star lore can be felt
in this world

in premonitions or
starry prescience.

This


you learned in righteous onrush and
sacred drudgery both. An ongoing commitment, a
long song convergence, a
*liturgical ambush.*


○

Uranus's collaboration with Nemesis in the outer reaches.
Saint Valentine's Day, 2011. Uranus transit, in perfect 180-degree opposition.
   That
radically heightened anticipatory
impulse.
      You are in
a large and spacious house, the house of
your father, lying in bed on the first
floor. The house, unusually well-lighted, begins
to fill with water. This is not a problem. Brilliant
wings of fire flare in the current while all around
in great and inspiring size, ancient fish and creatures of the sea
lumber and move as you
lie there.
      An Aquarian era's Permian luxuriance.
                               Even so,
you feel a poem coming together, the first, best summoning
of a poem you've long imagined but never
successfully begun but which, in that moment, you
feel the full force of. You can even
feel the elusive first line coming into expression
at that decisive moment. You feel that you must,
whatever the cost, draw this first line
out into life.

An auditorium.
A bathhouse.
Different kinds of public spaces.

An owl's nostril a fluid seeps from. New knowledge
it portends. The *Red Book's*
Uranian augur.
*The Labyrinth*, whose cover you saw
in your sleep.
                    The greatest poem ever written, the certainty
of which transmitted to you is only available
in outer night, vision
of a heavenly form you only find
as feeling; memory's
aroma.


The allure of your own auroral dream world.


You with your undistempered intellect—
see these Promethean teachings concealed beneath the veil
of this poetry carried directly across
to you

from mouth
to ear, from
mind
to eye.


                        ○


   Anthropic and theic, one mother, one
breath, creation's theurgical pneumatography fire unchains—
power. Raw

calcareous power
brazen Uranian endurance
fuels.

      But the gods are greater, mythically and
actually. Until.
                       Pheromones
urge your imagination, divine mirrors
sheening nature's silvery residue, its
deathless ephemarion. Eidetic, trans-
mutative, fate's
dromenon plays it that like the thief with the gift of fire,
you will be running furtively until the end of time.


A jeering jay's vagabond call.
A jet sneering the distant sky to tatters.
Magic.
Magic and all the concealed arts.
They have ravished you.


                           ○


"I was hallucinating mushrooms." A statement
of vision.


You were hallucinating ether, the angelic archways.
You were envisioning the magic forms. The condemnations of sorcery the
   elders
insisted on.

You were hallucinating human energy, seeing it as forms of flame.
You were hidden in the halls of night, the heavenly
enclosures. You were praying for the distant
forms. Saying and doing
the unusual things.

Earth's wrath's heart
stripped of rages and envies.

○

Uranus's extravagant epsilon ring
bright as a silver circlet
surrounding its luminous turquoise orb
visible against a background of
stars and moons.

March 1782. William Herschel spots Uranus through his telescope.

1800 million miles from the Sun.
Eighty-four years to complete its slightly elliptical orbit.
Every forty-two years, because of its axial inclination at
ninety-seven degrees, one of Uranus's poles is
pointing to the Sun while
the opposite pole is in darkness
for decades, its
rocky core
surrounded by a mantle of ice

topped by an atmosphere of hydrogen and helium
with two percent methane, giving
the planet its slight greenish color.

Uranus's buoyancy remains to be tested—
given its density it likely would sink in your ocean
if your ocean's volume expanded one
hundred times

to allow for
swallowing an outer
planet whole.

Uranus's homoerotic allure the arrival
of the new zodiac year announced
right as you were born. No wonder
your love of the art is defined
by men loving men
as a glamour
of time.
          The mysteries
of Uranus cannot be guessed at—
they have to be experienced.

The Uranian *visio spiritualis*
the guardian cherubim entwined in an embrace
resembling celestial sexual union
cored in fire, in

Promethean flame—.

From

the moment Saturn castrated Uranus—locked from your birth in perfect
    opposition—the sky

has never once again joined the earth in union.

Forever separated, time

is an antique

orbital curl.

*Uranus's manhood cast violently into the sea*
*but foaming aphroditically to life.*

O

Wayfaring wren in the newly pruned lilac.

Renovations of Chaldean magic.

Doctrines of stellar astrology

circulated in a period of terminal despair. Who

are the heralds who render your physical death inoffensive

by announcing the mystical, initiatory death

even the Prophet

sighed at the onset of.

Is the Tree of Life

subject to seasonal death? How

do the leaves that fall from its branches nourish the soil

where your burial will happen?

The flourishes of your life—foreseen in

gigantic orbital forms—will at last
be consumed to be passed on
anew.

○

On the field of action, thrashed
to its perimeters with lightning, a lashing mental gush.

○

Uranus's theophanic immateriality, his revolutionary
uplift. His anomalous
retrograde tilt.

What revolution? To resist the melancholy lake
of alcohol pooling from Saturn's
inherited woes, to reject
the pull of the abyss for
the scattered stars obeying higher
                    forms.
                            You
settle for studied rebellion. Or do you?
It involves reading, usually early, page after page, the pour
of light from the lamp. You dive in—the depths
teem with esotericism,
creatures,

defiance. God's
wrathful water bruin, intent
on evil, a Leviathan's
rippling flesh as
a wicked current bends in. A fantasy. Books.
Deep dives. Suffocating breath. But the uncanny allure.
You keep diving down, keep forcing oxygen
deeper into that Uranian transmission of the deeper, outer forms.

○

*What Prometheus knows is a secret.* Buried
in your heart. An enduring match flame: a poem
makes and unmakes
the world.

And the world
meteorizes
time.

Later, but not much later, he wrote you, "I'm
dying." The reverberating stereometric body you had
grown into and come alive through
slumped in collapse. You were helpless
with care, a whole continent, an entire
ocean away from him,
reduced to telegraphic transmissions—short

letters, expensive
telephone calls. But you spoke. And you told him
for the first and only time
that you loved him.

And when he died, some of the yeast
of your imagination was lost. No. Not
some. The nature of things was unleavened. How
long did it take for things to rise again? A decade. Exactly
how long he told you it would take
to become a poet.

Your daemonic power's onset's
righteous un-
raveling's re-
leavening.

○

*Uranian hymn.*

Just as the divine can only be manifest to your mind
if God reveals it; and just as your eyes
perceive the forms of the world when they are illuminated
by the Sun; just so, whoever
resolves to cultivate revelation must also
cultivate patience for Uranus's

reappearance in the midst of
every eighth decade otherwise lived
in apocalyptic darkness. God

constantly guards and mediates your life but
Uranus transmits its most
dynamic messages, hard to understand but
mantled in revolutionary truth. Theologians
of antiquity, whose memory you revere, read
Uranus's distant allure as Saturnine rumor, as
Aquarian expansion, the outer limit of things they
were only barely beginning to intuit, felt as motion, expansion, a

fore-echo of
oracle.

            They
conspired to see
what was hidden from them in an
anticipation of magical form—Zoroaster
adopted Arimapsis in his search
for the holy mysteries; Hermes
Thrice Greatest chose Aesculapius to whom
he described the gash
in the light the darkness seeps from; Thracian
Orpheus chose Museus to limn
the mysticism of violence with; and Aglaphemos found

Pythagoras in the celestial auditorium where
the starch of the stars dusts the strings
of the heavenly instruments. Thus
have the wise always found it necessary to have God

as their guide but a friend
as their companion.

You
are no sage
of antiquity nor
mystic master of time and
space. Your

manifold confusions are
psychodynamic absorptions, spectral
omphallisms, repeated
episodes of worry.
Nevertheless,

you keep searching
for truth's transmissive vectors
and find joy in questing
friends: von Hempel, the Elf, and Polyrhythms
among them.

○

Allegorize what fades from view.
Manifest the inadequate.
Enact the shapeless.
Follow the goddess.

FROM THE SPECTACLE

OF YOUR IMAGINATION,

ITS MYSTICAL LANCING

A scorpion,
water,
hibernal dawn:

Pressure the powers with far-flung sadness.
In whose sting will your own work throb?

# POWERS OF DISSOLUTION
# AND ABSORPTION

The ocean's aortal outer power.
Who is the worst force in the mind's
cloven ecosystem? What's
the unity that arises otherwise? Neptune's
seraphic focus. Angels outside time in perfect
motionlessness.

Jove's inventive wrath's celestial shortfall: rain.
His sea brother's auxiliary inundations he needs. Riverine
convocations tyrannical commands oblige: *Rivers of the world! Time
is short. I won't harangue. I won't
insult you.*
*Burst forth surge down crash through*
*the gates that hold you in,*
*flume*
*where the world*
*won't let you, let*
*your river horses*
*stampede!*

The mouths of the waters wide open.
The course to the sea unbridled.


With his trident, Neptune
strikes the heart of Earth's archaic wrath, percussing
its liquid core—tremoring
at the stroke and unsealing
oceanic floods. Earth and sea, sky and water, all
one, coursing wildly crashing all over you
the stars' resplendent mysticism, their
endowments, their pursuits. Heaven's shining enshrines
kindled sacrificial flames in the night sky the oceans
innumerably reflect—downward depth and
upward radiance. Your soul
                        is a sparkling particle
                                            upheaved
to the cosmic fires.


                    If nature had given to this legion
powers in kind with its strength, the Empyrean's subliming ethers
would be helpless before its flame
and the sky ablaze would consume the whole
universe.
            The marvels of nature produce on you a
mysterious impression. The view of immensity
elevates you above vulgarities. This feeling, innate
in you, astral religion has seized upon whose
theologians and magi celebrate the intensity of such that

material delights can seem
contemptible and
insipid.

Instead the solemn orb.
Instead the moonless night of stellar depths.

What bullshit!
Even so, you love it, the prog-rock
liner notes of it. Every word.

Now listen to this tale of astromantic woe.

○

DISSOLUTION

Vienna.
Peering from the nearly eroded edge
of the twentieth century, whose dreams
in bacterial writhings have worried
somatic homeostasis into its lurid
exalted corruptions, there—the edge
holds but the body
crumples in defeat—and there
you slumped, the abyss of the twenty-first century
yawning down from time devouring

downward. Dissolution, Viennese style: epic, Freudian, dainty,
civilized—:
        You went
to the opera where
                you sat next to an aged dowager,
her forearm jangling with excessive charms on a
gold chain, who in unison with Wotan
dismissed the entire nineteenth century with the flick
of a wrist and a single word,
"Geh."


      If only you *could* go!
Your collapse was to be worse than you could have imagined.


○


Dissolution has terrified you
since boyhood, even earlier, since
the time you were an infant when
ensnared in an esophageal web you
breathed under a tent of oxygen. Anxiety
has always been concentrated in your throat. And then
there was that time at the age of two you
wandered around the corner from your house all of a sudden
lost, recognizing nothing, a panic setting in until
by some miraculous string of memory you were
led back to the familiar. Your

hold on the world—always
slipping. At the end of the cycle of the visionary clock, its
ethereal dissolve, its secretive
motions, its unanticipated, penetrative
sting.

There aren't enough ways for you to handle Neptune's factors. Or
the scorpion's watery flense. Shrewd and regenerative, the poisonous
creature injects its venom
into your dissolving
religious imagination and you can hardly
orient yourself in the antique, subaqueous labyrinth
that most psychologically vexing city
on the planet had prepared
for you to get lost in
on the cusp of your first
Saturnine return.

You even shipped over copies of
the Standard Edition to stand sentinel
over your collapse. Their powder-blue spines
aligned on your bedroom's
shelves.

There you were, falling
apart in Vienna, the boundaries
of your person liquid, leaking self

incessantly like
some

delicious Freudian irony—. Do you remember
visiting the grand chapel at the sanatorium on the outskirts
of the city? Designed by Otto Wagner in his
most thoughtful Secession style. There were murals,
straight lines, light pouring
through beautiful figural and
abstract stained glass, these designed by Kolo Moser. Could you
have stayed there and found
the care you needed? Doubtful. But that
was the desperate *Zauberberg* fantasy. Anyways, you had her care at
every turn, even when you couldn't breathe
and she took you to the hospital to let the doctor
reassure you that you were fine. Why
didn't she leave you? It's amazing to think of. But of course
she was too busy holding you together
to go.

○

INTERLUDE

Centaurs—
their bluer surfaces and
more freshly exposed
ice.

Centaurs are
trans-Neptunian objects racing
through space scattered inwards, most likely
from close encounters with Neptune's prodigious
gravity. *Further interactions with giant planets*
*nudge the Centaurs inwards until*

*they become short-period comets, spending perihelion in*
*the inner solar system where*
*they are heated by the Sun and lose their volatiles*
*in sometimes spectacular tails.*

○

ABSORPTION

Neptune's outer-aqueous dissolves, his liquid hand in your own
falling apart. So strange that you fell apart, isn't it? But also
impossible that it didn't
somehow happen. Around
this disintegrating core, you'd been
circling since you were a boy—so how
did you pull yourself together again? What menace,
unthought but known, dispersed in the act
of your pulling it
together? Who
pulled?

The Living All. None other. Seraphic and enduring.

The ongoing feeling in your thoughts, the indissoluble forms,
*keeping their upward flight like great*
*slow-moving birds.*

This, perhaps, the thing most vivid for you
as you move ever more fully
into unity.

○

In your dream, as in a homily of Ælfric's, you find
a ghostly intelligence of
allegory and prefiguration, prospects
of time's unwinding in water. You're
buoyed in choppy currents, riverine and rapid, coursing
swiftly among the towers
of a great city, cut by waterways, bobbing
with a speed only partly in control, moving
where the rapid current pulls you.

Hued in methane, luculent blue and erratic, the sorcerer
of the outer reaches inspiring
you and your oneiric crew
urged you
to drop the oars in the waters
and pull without ceasing before the avalanching wall

of the storm's roaring onset. Raging winds. Cerulean
hurricanes. The inhospitable sea you and your crew of fools
row on. Neptune tends this
watery patch

proclaiming it holy. Away, on land, by the shoreline, an altar:
three dozen heifers with hides of unblemished red
crowd around where priests
with blades newly sharpened await
the murderous portent: lightning's
eruptive laceration and
atmospheric
spilth.
And you, pulling onward
into deeper peril, cry out
to the Lord of Storms and Ships, that you might
be spared from the
                    *irresistible onset of the crashing rocks:* Death.
The fear of death locks you in an ice of the outer writhe, alive
but convinced that death is the name
of the bottomless well
of the real.

Neptune's dissolving infinities. How
do you feel about the onset of death? About
the cycle's end? What other worlds, watery and obscure, do you sense
in the vastness, in the slow blue curl
of the outer reaches? Eternity

spills out from the terminus thought
thrills to feel the arrival of,
fully formed but already vanishing
into a fantasy of star tilth, the zodiac's mansions a series
of furrows, your horoscope's dark
ecology a mystical
blur . . .

○

Neptune's oceanic extent whose depths reflect
your imaginal system's spectral umber—everything
you know but aren't at this moment thinking; everything
once known but now forgotten; everything you've ever
felt, even what's gone unnoted; everything autonomously you've
felt, thought, remembered, wanted done; and every future thing
taking shape in this matrix, the form into which all your experience
is poured and will sometime later
reveal itself—all
water, deep
water.
    *Night*
*is Earth's shadow between the Sun and you*
*dreaming* an ocean of unreckoned knowing flows from
vast and dark, you

but a "fringe of consciousness" whose sunlight
the rings of Neptune
only poorly reflect.

○

Neptune's surprising signature scrawled
in watery weaves of
gravity and deep space.

You
spectral in habitation
of the twelfth and most dolorous
mansion, a dream

coiled around your heart, the thorn
of its stinger at rest where
the valve of an arterial throb controls
the revelation, soaked in truth and achronical
with your soul's
simultaneities

that would otherwise already
overwhelm you.

○

The ripeness of death Neptune's methane hue symbolizes, the feeling
of immortality you're incapable
of rationalizing—*a peculiar feeling of extension
in time and space*—deification,
its ritual timbres where darkness
booms its depths.

When

have you felt absorbed into God? Whose

eternal house shelters all the living stars?


The unintegrated absorption of reading. Pure fantasy.

The St. Clair River's constant gushing surge, racing

downriver on a speed boat, skipping

from shifting tip to scooped trough

along the current, the great curved blade of the autumn Sun

swinging diagonally ahead. *The Four Seasons*

when the floor dissolved from under you. Wading

up the river in the slot canyon in Zion. The Cooper's hawk

heraldic in the gingko at dusk. And the snowy owl in the deep frost's

high-pressure darkness furling down like a cloud of silence and

soaring effortlessly on. The orchid boat.

Every time. Oars in the water

pulling to shore, plying the endless ripples

annihilation's sweet release

issues onward. Patmos.

The Monastery of Apocalypse. The cave's ceiling's trinal sutures

the holy strike of lightning left there—seeing that.

All the icons elucidating that

fulgurating flash. Saints


who stain the gold with life even whose brilliance

can't absorb it utterly. You've felt life most

around the dinner table, no one

particularly caring for the effort gone into

making the meal, your quaternity temporarily
unified, the four-fold alchemy linking you
together, green and blue and yellow and orange
harmonizing, differential, zoomorphic, good. Even

Neptune and the horses he commands
approach the table gently,
giving thanks.

○

At last, Neptune's display of images on the outermost screen of the stars—
*soul-confusing, soul-absorbing, soul-consuming*
shapes from dreams—hazardous
to see without the spiritual
mind Neptune's oceanic depths require—

what is true of art and dream
is also true of mystical experience, when your soul
is raised up from the visible realm
to where what is seen fades, dissolves

and the currents of the invisible
start leaking everywhere so that you slide
in its streams. But one image you cling to,
threading your fingers in its weave—: a fabric of time
and space in whose taut meshes and
undular fold you're a visible thread of

fleeting significance otherwise
anonymously woven in a quantum garment whose
vital raiment clothes you

in thinking and seeming, radiant with
appearance's meaning.

                    The same
uplift that elevates your vision plunges
you in doubt and dissimulation while Neptune,
swiftly spinning, its crystalline ring argenteous with distant sunlight, curls
slowly out of sight into fathomless
darkness.

Adhere then
to the vision
and its one
pneumatic
thrum.

FROM THE SPECTACLE

OF YOUR IMAGINATION,

ITS TERMINAL SIGH

At the moment of your birth, at long distance, the earnest nonorientable fact of your heavenly influence: destructive, erosive, conclusive.

# ECOPHANIC TERRORS

## THE SEVEN-HEADED DRAGON

Stone
upon
stone
thrown
down

time's
doom
ungiants
in
a wild
defiance
of wars
rumors of wars
earthquakes and famines—
birth pangs—

signs and prodigies
to lead you astray:

In the oceanic darkness of the heliopause, a sea monster, a
chaos monster, creation's worst
enemy—

*draco magnus et rufus*—

the seven-headed red dragon of synchronic
history, Pluto's apocalyptic
monstrosity

the slicks of whose forked tongue
are tattooed upon your palms, incidentally
divining your
destiny. Pluto's

enormous wealth and your
ensuing destitution

(emotionally speaking).


FILLING YOU WITH EVIL


Since the Apocalypse
you now know again that God
is not only to be loved but also to be feared.
He fills you with evil as well as with good, otherwise
he would not need to be feared; and because

he wants to become a man, the uniting of his conflicting laws
must take place in a man. Imagine
a new responsibility. You
can no longer wriggle out of things on the plea
of your littleness and nothingness,
for the Dark God has slipped nuclear and chemical weapons
into your hands atwitch with nervous energy
and giving you the power to pour out apocalyptic vials of wrath
on all your fellow creatures, flushing them
in cataclysm.
Since you have been granted
an almost godlike power, you can
no longer remain blind and unconscious.
You must like the serpent coiled around a biblical tree
know something of God's nature and the supernatural powers
if you are to understand yourself
and to find in the sinus of the divine
some enfolded texture, some fingered pattern
you can bear back to the world of light
and wave there like a flag, either a signal or a surrender.
But perhaps both.


THE FIRE


Divinized by the fire that is to re-cast you, the fire
that will consume you and fulfill
you. To be consumed
and to be transfigured

are one and the same.

The intractable surface of Pluto's far-distant influence, its
cheerless limits where
penniless ghosts wait forever
on the Stygian banks and where

Hellish dogs devour
ghostly fugitives and living souls—Pluto,

who is fierce and jealous of his rights, who
seldom visits the upper air
except when on business or when
lust overtakes him—nymphs
he has violated
transformed into white poplars clinging
to the edge of the pool
of memory

in Hell's
deepest
well.

Visions
of the seven-headed
fire-hued
dragon—
slits

in the sky
the lightning of its revelation
flames through.

Devourer.
Deceiver and contemptible
consumer only curses and oaths
invoke

pouring out horror and woe
Pluto's lorn course marks the shape of: another
wonder in heaven, a

seven-headed sign of
wealth in excess leaving

the world in depleted ruin
wasted for any renewing vision

you might summon to fill
the caverns and fissures in Hell's
gravity pools.

Creation's worst enemy.

Sheddings of blood and diminutions—belittle
the flame-hued dragon free and wreaking
such havoc, flouting such

wrong. You're
standing by, offering up the knife
with which your wrists are to be slit.

Of peaceful and wrathful deities no sign—
only the dragon's undular writhes and smoke
and the land and the sky on fire.

These are the last days
and this is what they feel like
and this is the dragon that makes all things rue . . .

THE FORTRESS OF HISTORY

No mystery, you pilgrims of the latter days—the heads
of the dragon are politicians, one
worst of all—flame-hued with
sham vigor, fatuous force—but all
incalculably awful, wicked
destroyers, Earth's and love's
plunderers, toxic
beyond all endurance, ruiners
whose heads atwist atop their
writhing necks wrack
all things for the pleasure of it. And you,
you're in their thrall, watching the seven heads
of the great beast move, its great tail curl, its

154

colossal body crawl. You can't
take your eyes from the dragon, can't
imagine any life without its serpentine form
occupying your agitated core where
all sense and meaning
have been reduced to flickers and pulsations of
a perplexing Plutonic
horror.

○

The forests of history have burned to the ground.
You are helping with the arson of inaction
to burn all the forests of history
down
to the ground.

SHOCK AT THE HELIOSHEATH

Pluto's avid flirtation with the liminal zone—
the sheet between your solar world and
interstellar space—

where blasting winds that move nearly
two million miles per hour
crash into the terminal shock where
they slow below the speed of sound. Here

155

eased solar winds coil
into the interstellar medium that shapes
the heliosheath which extends outward for
many millions of miles. In this zone
of the Sun's exuded potency, to which Pluto and Charon
in their orbital covenant bear distinct witness, you
come at last

to the legendary sphere of the fixed stars—

the dark sheet's solar umbra through which
you see those
stellar pinpoints as still as animals
at rest on your antique
convictions. The universe

conforms to the world, not
the world to the universe.


FORMS OF PHYSICAL MYSTICISM

Pluto's metalless presciences the world obliquely observes—
What will happen to the world? All
of your powers have prepared you to
make a prediction but
still you do not know. In-
stead, you sense

dark marks, ultra-
violet radiations, disturbances
in the vegetable life of men
and women.

From dreams, from
discredited Church reports,
from an outer planetary phosphorescence, cold
as winter's dawn.

Consider the salamandrine woman
suspended for more than a
half hour above a fiery brazier
enveloped in a simple sheet while
neither she nor the wrapping
were consumed
in flame. Stig-

matization, elevation above the ground
in prayer, celestial radiance, emanations
of perfume, blood portents after death—
these miracles, impressive though they were in
ages past, work
worthless mercies
in our ruined
world Pluto's menacing
outcast motions

epochally
circumscribe.

Bodily elongations—physical
manifestations—there's nothing to do
but watch them happen and wish
they might improve
your wasted realm but
they won't. It's

merely
your circus.

It's falling apart.
It's falling apart.
A great wave is building
out beyond the edge of the visible
to break upon the land.

What can you say?
What will you say? Fling

the emptiness into the coursing airwaves
and gather what you can
from the incoming
influence: Plato's

enchiridion on the apocalypse—
destructive upheavals

widespread social and political change (all the fools in jail)

massive empowerment of evil and good

rebellious impulses

technocracy unlimited

revolts

and nearly evaporated

convictions, including your core truth:

a more complete contact with God

lies in the future.


## THE ARGUMENT OF THE SUN

*The ark of the lymbe betwixe his aux, that is now in Cancer, and the blake*
*thred, is the argument of the same. The ark betwixe the blake thred and*
*the white in the lymbe is the equacion of the sonne, which ark is but litel.*
(John Westwyk, *The Equitorie of the Planetis*)


Pluto's orbital resonance with Neptune is the equation of the Sun.

Pluto's demotion to planetoid is the argument of the Sun.

Pluto's eventual demolition of time with the Sun's colossal blessing is your

  thought's most icy fringe.

Consider Christ's realized eschatology.

Consider Christ's apocalyptic preaching. Were these

incidental? Were these not

premonitions of

Pluto's outer limit's

archaic dolor's rueful color?

What shall be the sign when all these things
will begin to be
consummated?
     Exsurgent
earthmovings and great blindings. Realm
against realm.

Troubles.
Famishments.

Woe's precognitive *ymagion*, loquacious and loosed.
You are not the speaker but the Holy Ghost.
You and your brother will deliver your brother to death.
Kings and queens and doomsmen you shall stand before.
If you endure to the end, you shall be saved.

Brief days in the scheme of days.
Succorless trials.

Omnipredictive visions
in dark words of the Sun's dark waxing,
of the Moon's lightless end and the stars'
ultimate exhaustions:

the moving powers' paralysis, locked
for time's end.

Clouds.
Gathering glory.
Little puffs of power.
Incessant groaning from the highest
thing in heaven.

What ointment might soothe the ache?
What dawning finds the vision alive?

Over-ripened figs.
In handfuls, in bushels.

What daunting falseness do you need revealed to
see what was written for you and held
with such matchless care
since the time the planets were first glimpsed
in their tracks, inscribing the sky
with destiny?

Look up!
*Vigilate*!
Pray!

You are it and
that's all
you can see.

Pluto's transformative fervor's allure
lost in hostile inertia
and dereliction—
jet fuel's pollutions, plutocrats'
ruling apathies, your
perfect absorption into a small glowing
rectangle—every

change that you're making leads you
further into ruin.

Consumed in horoscopic doubt a
cataclysmic vision of a dying ecocosm
nevertheless
arises—what
otherworldly being accords you this
intervening vision? Whose vertical journey
is spiking through your spinal
column? This vision
contains no luxuriant temples
cooled in celestial breezes, no symbols
of cosmic phenomena or menageries of fantastic beasts, no
Beatrice announced by magnificent griffons
promising deliverance, no mysterious numbers either,
no spectral escorts, no
liturgical ambush,

no flashes of light in irisized
splendor—

it's just this: decadence
and debauchery; active evil advocated
as decency; sham government;
a dying planet; the last days of democracy—.

Who knew at the moment of your birth, when
Pluto began from its watchful perch in midheaven
its incremental curl from noon
towards the strained light of dawn, that
you would lose the insight
to tell the awfulness
of the swallowing of the scroll
from the conclusive emancipation
that consumption
portends?

Pluto's involutionary underbeginning
in the netherworld's
unregenerate echolalia.
                        Pluto's
evolutionary undertaking
in the upper world's
esoteric
redemptions.

163

When the planet is working through its darker nature, you
are drenched in astromantic
ruin
eroding the mantle of the telluric
unconscious realm. When the planet
is working through its beneficial nature, you're drawn
to regenerate what's

been forewrecked
or to call
for an active witness
to all this
doom, this wreckage.
The paralysis of instinct Pluto implodes in you
and your kin.
                Pluto's inaudible lower octave—so low, so
remote, you can't
make it out.

In an ancient chronicle, Alfred sayeth:
Our elders loved wisdom. When you
look to where they lived, you see it
and through that wisdom they gained wealth and bequeathed it to us. Look:
You can see in time their swath,
but you won't follow in their footsteps after them.

And look now: You've abandoned their
wisdom and wealth because you will not bend down

on the track that they made
with your mind.

Pluto licks his yellowing chops and you
stumble to serve him some more of your foolishness.

        Moses's face
so radiant with divine presence
that on coming down from Sinai its brightness
terrified the Israelites. So Moses
veiled his face
whenever he addressed the people.

Scripture is a veil.
Revelation is a mirror.

Plutonic depth is a veil of darkness;
apocalypse a sudden illuminating splashdown
in the Kuiper Belt's
outer
reaches.

CONSUMPTION AND TRANSFIGURATION

All things have lore
and form

among themselves
and this

is the shape that makes the universe
resemble God

true even
when the shape of things to come

augurs all endings—
languages, cultures, people weakened

by the woes of living,
civilizations,

species, ecosystems,
zodiacs—

all forms of life Pluto's slowly enacted oracle foreknows and owns
a hibernal snow settles on
and ensouls.
              Divinized

by the fire that is to re-cast you, the fire
that will consume you and fulfill
you. To be consumed
and be transfigured

are one and the same thing.

What if Pluto's underworld
with its extensive morbid riches
is an outer world fringed in heliopause
beyond which in expanding cold
the unknown
in whose formless totality the forces
of your life
were born
clasps the stars fixed in the night
unstilling their shapes in defiance of any
destiny inscribed there?

# CODA

The ether's fateful unstillnesses time's
daemonic designs ripple through
underbeginning
the shape
your life
allows
free you to see through the fuzzed
aura your life's daily disturbances
grow from its
invisible core:

Looking out, what did you notice?
Looking in, what did you learn?

You saw the planets' radiant lines of force like gears in clockwork wind an
    anticipatory synchrony.
You saw your birth star, neither lucky nor cursed, hung in the sky at the
    point where night is deepest.
You saw the Sun in total eclipse shudder in an ecstasy of archangelic
    premonition.
You saw the Moon's unanalyzable residuum, like a mood, like a master-
    piece, like the soul's own movements.

You saw the light of the stars waxing and waning, exhilarations and omens
   no routines of speculation can augur entirely.
You saw stellar principalities and apostles of learning worry where the
   world is turning.

You learned the Holy Spirit's zodiac coruscation creation's alleluias
   circumcinct.
You learned that the panther, the lion, and the she-wolf menacing your way
   are vehicular and fluxional—a portion of vision.
You learned from Pythagoras and Plato that the soul encinders the body
   and that whatever you do or suffer here is the beginning of the blaze.
You learned the study of the stars prepares you for another existence your
   worldly transience merely suggests.
You learned the doctrine of sidereal immortality and you shuddered at its
   abyssal ravishments.
You learned that the Earth, beaten and betrayed, is brighter than any
   star, better than any fate, more epic than any autobiography, more
   sympathetic than any magic.

And what, at last, did you do?

You copied the stars' wonderworking craft
that canopies the world—
its wastes and ruins and
match-lit glories—
and whose manifold shapes
prefigure
your passion

and to this work you brought gold and silver and
dearworth gemstones
and the hair of a goat
just as God has bid.

# A HARMONY

(YEATS 2019)

The joy of heaven is continual battle.
Its multitudinous influxes
you monitor. No one

desired the strife you've endured;
no one worried about the ruining
shame. Instead, your vision hurtles forward

with the sages' dispensations where
one status cedes to the next
to be devoured at last

by the dragon of flame whose secret
lawgiver is the Holy Spirit
and whose glimmering doom is already warm—

ecosystemic
and doing harm.

173

# Glossary

aerarium: treasury

beleric myrobalan: a deciduous tree that grows in India

chronism: the condition of a being's (or group's) relation to time

chronocrator: Saturn; sometimes, following his usurpation of power, Jupiter. Ruler of Time

cryovolcanic: a cryovolcano erupts methane and ammonia, rather than molten rock. Venus's volcanoes are cryovolcanic

dodecatropaic: twelve-fold turning; a coinage

dynamolosis: in this context, a coinage for the process of revealing/releasing energy

ecophanic/ecophany: a coinage for when an environment manifests itself to you on its own—non-human—terms. What theophany is to God, ecophany is to an environment

Empyrean: ultimate realm of fire, the Tenth Ptolemaic Sphere, the heavens beyond the spheres generally

enchiridion: a small book or handbook, often containing essential information

ephemarion: something passing quickly away (coinage)

eophoric: carrying the dawn

escharot: dead tissue

exioherari: alchemical term for "holy sperm"

furibund: frenzied, raging

*Geh*: German for "Go!"

heliopause: the boundary where the Sun's onrushing solar wind ceases as it meets the interstellar medium of stellar winds from surrounding stars pushing back

heliosheath: the region of the heliosphere beyond the termination shock. This is where the solar winds slow and compress as they meet the interstellar medium. It is combined within the heliopause but beyond the Kuiper Belt, where the solar system ends.

heresiarch: a founder of a heresy; ruler of a heretical sect

horolation: rotation around an ideal point

hypaethral: open to the air

kraterion: ruler

lithosphere: the rigid outermost sphere of a terrestrial planet or satellite

lunium: the notional lunar space surrounding a planet (coinage)

precession: denotes the retrograde motion of the Vernal Point through the constellations, so that, for instance, over time the first point of tropical Aries seems to retrograde—move backwards—through the constellations

*Primum Mobile*: the Ptolemaic Ninth Sphere that imparts movement to all the other spheres

*Quellgeist*: "source spirit" (from Böhme)

rypophagous: filth-eating

selenoscope: any device used for looking at the Moon

selenodont: mythical moon-beast

spectroscopy: the study of the interaction between matter and electromagnetic radiation, as light in a prism

synaxis: a gathering of the faithful in liturgy (Orthodoxy)

*tigersprung*: "a tiger's leap": a word used by Walter Benjamin to describe how fashion can leap from modern to ancient and back again to the contemporary

tungol: star (Old English)

Uranus transit: planetary transits involve positioning the planets at any given time in relation to an individual's natal chart. Transiting Uranus, specifically the personal transit of Uranus opposite Uranus, meaning the point at which Uranus finds itself in 180 degrees opposition to where Uranus appears on the natal chart, is something that happens between your fortieth and fiftieth years (which variation is owed to

Uranus's elliptical eighty-eight-year orbit) and that can coincide with a period in life in which inner experience and external events powerfully converge, according to Richard Tarnas. My Uranus transit occurred on February 14, 2011.

vastagonal: a coinage for Zeus's colossal orthography

zedoary: a rhizomatic plant with medicinal properties

# Afterword

*(A)strology . . . is what produces the aptitude for visionary apperception of the suprasensory worlds, these being manifested by the figures and constellations which shine in the skies of the soul, the Sky of the Earth of Light.* —Henry Corbin, *The Man of Light in Iranian Sufism*

*The Hidden Eyes of Things* completes a trilogy on modes of consciousness, begun in *Phosphorescence of Thought*, a book-length poem about the evolution of consciousness, and continued in *Earth Is Best*, a serial poem that uses foraging for wild mushrooms to explore altered states of consciousness. *The Hidden Eyes of Things* uses the discipline of astrology to explore the unconscious.

Why astrology? In *The Interpretation of Dreams*, Freud wrote, "The belief held in antiquity that dreams were sent by the gods in order to guide the actions of men was a complete theory of dreams, giving information on everything worth knowing about them." The same is true of astrology, which—along with alchemy—is the most legible esoteric system, even whose most cryptic operations speak somehow meaningfully to the imagination. Astrology, especially in its ancient form, is a complete theory of the soul, whose daemonic aspirations and perturbations become known through its grammar of revelation. "For the soul," wrote Marsilio Ficino in the *Book of Life*, "builds figures with its reasons beyond the stars in heaven."

Astrology avails the experience and metaphoric power of projection. Internal realities—emotions, thoughts, dreams—are projected out of the self involuntarily and without interruption onto the external world. What is inchoate and incoherent inside is at least as chaotic outside but for the ceaseless action of that projection, which is cast ultimately on the screen of the stars where spread into patterns, your interiority

179

now on display begins to take shape—mythical, dramatic, archetypal shape—and thus objectified and recognizable begins the long and vivid process of precipitating back into your interior self, but this time as empirical truth, with notable texture and form.

Though astrology is daemonic, it is not fatalistic. What you see in the planets and the stars doesn't determine your fate. Rather, in an actualization of the Heraclitean oracle—*ethos anthropo daimon*—astrology bodies character forth in a magnificent and minute clockwork dialing the heavens into finer attunements depending on how subtly you wish to adjust it. Your horoscope—clock seeing/time seeing—specifically your natal horoscope—uses the positions of the planets at the moment of your birth and diagrams them in such a way as to show large-scale relations and trends, including conjunctions, oppositions, trines, squares, and the places of the planets in their celestial mansions. (Some may note that I am writing here in general about tropical astrology.)

How does astrology work? You could say that it doesn't work; rather, it reveals things about your character based on the celestial placement of the Sun, the Moon, and the other planets at the moment of your birth and thereafter in relation to the planets' present positions. Galileo, who like Newton, Ficino, Dante, and Milton knew astrology cold, wrote to Grand Duke Cosimo de' Medici:

> It was Jupiter, I say, who at your Highness's birth, having already passed through the murky vapors of the horizon, and occupying the midheaven and illuminating the eastern angle from his royal house looked down upon Your most fortunate birth from that sublime throne and poured out all his splendor and grandeur into the most pure air, so that with its first breath Your tender little body and Your soul, already decorated by God with noble ornaments, could drink in this universal power and authority.

"Of all the causes," wrote Plotinus, "the stars are the remotest." But they're also as "wandering stars" (or planets) unusually legible to us such that we keep looking to them for causes.

Astrology enacts human-planetary interdependences. Ptolemy's vision of the seven visible planets is the one we have inherited and continue to see with. Imagine a holarchy of nested transparent orbs into which each planet is lodged expanding outwards towards heaven itself. Dante climbed celestial ladders from one of these spheres to the next in the *Paradiso* until he reached the celestial rose. There were seven spheres, each corresponding to the seven planets known to the ancients because visible to the naked eye. In order, from nearest to farthest from Earth, they are the Moon, Mercury, Venus, the Sun, Mars, Jupiter, and Saturn. Traditionally, the influence of the Sun, Venus, and Jupiter has been regarded as benevolent (as evident in Galileo's letter to Cosimo de' Medici); the influence of Mars and Saturn has been regarded as malevolent; and the Moon and Mercury as ambivalent, meaning, strictly speaking, they can go either way, especially in combination with another planet. (The Moon traditionally rules the emotional life; Mercury the quicksilver aspect of the intellectual life.) Dante, like Milton, knew no other planets. And yet the Ptolemaic model expanded to the sphere of the fixed stars, then to the *Primum Mobile*, the sphere that sets the others in motion, and finally to the Empyrean, the realm of heavenly fire encompassing everything.

Though ancient in origin, the mythical archetypes of the seven planets to a Christian understanding of the cosmos were readily adapted by Christians, who assigned angelic regency to each of the planetary spheres. You encounter these assignments in the *Paradiso*, in which the traditional angelic hierarchies watch over the heavenly spheres. Angels rule the Moon, archangels rule Mercury, Principalities Venus, Powers the Sun, Virtues Mars, Dominations Jupiter, and Thrones Saturn. For the further spheres, Cherubim rule the fixed stars, and Seraphim rule the *Primum Mobile*. The Empyrean is God's realm.

In 1781, astronomer William Herschel discovered unusual motion among the stars in an exhaustive survey of the heavens he was conducting. It was Uranus. In 1846, observing perturbations in Uranus's orbit, mathematician Urbain LeVerrier predicted the existence of another planet beyond Uranus, confirmed that same year by Johann Galle. It was Neptune. On the basis of similarly observed discrepancies, astronomer Percival Lowell hypothesized the existence of a tenth planet, confirmed in 1930 by Clyde Tombaugh. This was Pluto. Modern astrologers include all three outer planets in their calculations, even despite Pluto's recent demotion to planetoid. Some of the

181

energies of the seven Ptolemaic planets have been redistributed among the outer planets, but more mysteriously, apocalyptically. They aren't so much malevolent or benevolent as epochal, because they move in such colossal orbits.

(In line with these discoveries, *The Hidden Eyes of Things* adheres to the traditional assignments of the angelic hierarchies, while assigning Cherubim to Uranus, Seraphim to Neptune, and Pluto's unfathomable outlook to the Empyrean.)

Is Mercury really mercurial? Is Saturn saturnine? I think, yes. What is mercurial in me—quite a lot, as it happens—is projected out of me where the placement of Mercury when I was born—in the third of the heavenly houses in the constellation of Pisces—reflects those qualities (communication and language, quickness of thought, a religiously and emotionally inflected intellect, for instance) and magnifies them for me to see. As astrologer Richard Tarnas puts it, "The nature of these [planetary] correlations presents to the astrological researcher what appears to be an orchestrated synthesis combining the precision of mathematical astronomy with the psychological complexity of the archetypal imagination, a synthesis whose sources seemingly exist a priori within the fabric of the universe." Jung is reported to have wished that if he had ten additional years, he would devote them to studying astrology.

I've been working on this poem for not quite so long, but I've been imagining it for almost that long, and its initial vision appeared to me more than a quarter of a century ago in a dream, which I related to Ronald Johnson in a letter I sent to him on April 27, 1994:

> I recently had a dream in which I was with a very mercurial professor of mine, who teaches the Fourth Gospel and incendiary readings of Paul's letters, and we were in a bookstore: he fetched a copy of *The Maximus Poems*, thanked me, and began looking for a poem, checking the "front index." I told him to check the back, for titles and first lines. He was very excited and didn't seem to know how use a poetry book. Then he found what he was looking for, a poem called "The Hidden Eyes of Things." All the while a mysterious unidentified third figure looked on as well as the old proprietor of the bookstore, which had been, at the dream's start, an abandoned warehouse.

182

I don't remember exactly when it occurred to me to write a poem or a book using this title, but my notebooks indicate ruminations that extend back for seven years or more. A new poem or project typically marinates in me for a few years before I begin to act. Once the writing began, it was totally absorbing, a visionary thrall. I wrote the sections in Ptolemaic order, from one planet to the next, climbing my way upwards and outwards to Pluto.

I've made use of several books over the course of composition. There's a complete list on my website, www.luxhominem.com, but I want to mention three books here. First, *The Arkana Dictionary of Astrology* by Fred Gettings. This book was given to me as a gift many years ago by my friend Harry Potter. He bought it for me at the Mayflower Occult Bookshop in Berkeley, Michigan, where the owner once accused me of stealing books by Madame Blavatsky (something I never did; I've never stolen a book in my life). This is an almost endlessly useful volume written with a depth of knowledge and insouciant care you wish every such comprehensive book was written with. Next is *Wonders of the Solar System* by astrophysicist Brian Cox. This book is a companion to a BBC series I've not yet seen. Wanting astronomic facts involved in each of the planetary sections of the poem, I found Cox's book—replete with photos and helpful diagrams—as companionable as it was helpful. And third, and above all, *Cosmos and Psyche* by Richard Tarnas, which is a Jungian-archetypal application of the recurrence of planetary transits, which refers to the crossing of a planet over any other planet's position in the heavens, and their impacts on world-historical events. Tarnas's book is visionary, keyed to the harmonics of the planets themselves, especially Uranus, whose influence he reads persuasively in light of the myth of Prometheus—the rebellious forerunner—rather than Saturn's even dourer father. All three books were as near at hand as the many notebooks I used while composing this poem.

Why astrology *now*? A progressively apocalyptic poem in apocalyptic times doesn't necessarily mitigate the apocalypse. But failing to imagine the apocalypse is to succumb to Nemesis, one of the seven lots in Greek astrology, the goddess of retribution and the augur of the endless night.

# *Acknowledgments*

Thanks to the editors of the publications in which sections of this poem appeared: Whit Griffin of *Blazing Stadium*, Kim Dorman of *Poetry at Sangham*, and Autumn Richardson and Richard Skelton of both *Reliquiae* and *Poetry and Nature* (Corbel Stone Press).

Stellar counsel and Eleventh-House magniloquence from Devin Johnston (water), Michael O'Leary (earth), John Tipton (earth), Stephen Williams (earth), Steven Toussaint (water), Pam Rehm (air), Nathaniel Tarn (water), and G.C. Waldrep (air).

At a mysterious impasse in the composition of this poem, specifically during Mars, I received a package—one of the best I have ever received—from Cody-Rose Clevidence, which contained a knife they had forged from an elevator cable, with a smooth walnut handle, exquisitely balanced. "The Blade" reflects that gift and is thereby dedicated to Cody-Rose.

In the celestial mansion, you will find a wing that extends for several rooms filled with art and objects, various and absorbing in their ways, mysterious technologies, and comfortable places to sit. At a table, with sheaves of hand-outs at the ready, you'll find Victoria Martin (air), who will instruct you and, always, keep watch over you, guiding you in this whole undertaking. Elsewhere in the mansion, you'll find an extraordinary library, with shelf after shelf lined with all the books you are interested in reading, in the center of which are three or four well-used and wonderfully comfortable couches, forming a rectangle, with coffee tables piled with books in the center. Off from the library is a doorway that leads into a kitchen bright with the light of the afternoon, the wood of the countertops and cabinets well-worn, an inviting table near the windows, a bowl of grapes in its center, crisp and agreeably sweet, and there's a chicken roasting in the oven, the aroma pluming everywhere, a crusty loaf on a cutting board waiting for dinner. Thomas Meyer (air) is there in the kitchen and everything he will show you will resemble the meal he is about to serve you—satisfying and companionable, full of love and kindness, served with endlessly, vibrantly intelligent talk, all of it like memory from an earlier life.

# PETER O'LEARY

was born in Detroit in 1968. He studied literature and religion
at the University of Chicago. He is the author of six previous
collections of poetry, as well as three collections of prose, including
*The Four Horsemen: Poetry and Apocalypse*, which is forthcoming.
He lives in Oak Park, Illinois and teaches at the School of the
Art Institute of Chicago. With John Tipton, he edits Verge Books.

○

FRONTISPIECE ILLUSTRATION BY THE AUTHOR

PUBLISHED BY THE CULTURAL SOCIETY

CULTURALSOCIETY.ORG

ISBN 978-0-9994912-7-0

DESIGNED BY CRISIS (EARTH)

PRINTED IN MICHIGAN ON

ACID-FREE, RECYCLED PAPER